WARNING!

Lots of crazy words!

Author: Matthew Hitch

Co-author: Sunok Moon

Illustrator: Matthew Hitch

Cover Design: Brittany Hitch

Layout Design: Matthew Hitch

Text Design: Matthew Hitch

Image Manager: Matthew Hitch

~~Vain Meglomaniac: Matthew Hitch~~

Credits Editor: Matthew Hitch

Image Manager Manager: S. Moon

Image Manager Manager Control: Absolutely no one

Artistic Arguer: Sunok Moon

Dishwasher: Matthew Hitch
(occasionally Sunok Moon)

Title: Captain Matt's Super Crazy Fun

Preschool Phonics 1 Student Book

ISBN 979-11-982546-5-8

First published 2023

Published by Hitch Publishing

info@supercrazyfun.net

This textbook came about as the result of 20 years of trying to make kids enjoy learning English. It is designed around the use of the rhotic R and other characteristics of English pronunciation common in North America. We believe it can be used in other parts of the world as most phonics books can, and we are keen to hear feedback from anyone who tries this.

We want to make clear that the word "crazy" used in the title is in relation to any of the common definitions illustrated below, and does not refer in any way to the meaning "insane."

strange/illogical   **wild**   **unexpected**   **fun**   **unwise**

About the Authors:

Matthew Hitch has taught English in Korea for the better part of 20 years and holds a master's degree in applied linguistics. He clearly does not have a pig nose, and by most accounts is not at all malodorous. He also cuts a dashing figure according to his wife.

Sunok Moon prefers to go by the name Michelle, and is in fact quite scary as reported in the bio on the back of this book. She has a degree in English literature and has taught English in Korea for approximately 3 weeks longer than Matthew, who is writing this and finds it weird to refer to himself in the third person.

Contents

Welcome parents and teachers!

Thank you for considering our book. Phonics books are notoriously boring, so this is the last bastion of publishing where even the tiniest bit of creativity can raise the bar (sorry phonics book publishers, but it's true). With that said, we humbly offer you our content. We have also intentionally challenged convention in a few ways. Much of what we have to say may be used or discarded though, and these books can be used just like any other mainstream phonics book. We hope you will choose to use whatever you please and dispose of the rest.

Please allow us to explain just where our method of teaching phonics may diverge from mainstream approaches, and please do forgive us for sharing information from what is undeniably the most mind-numbingly boring and seemingly useless field of study, linguistics. Most phonics books are not written by scholars in the field of linguistics. They are mostly written by early childhood educators, so perhaps that's the first divergence. We'll start with how we sound out consonants. In linguistic studies it is not uncommon for consonants to be distinguished by using a vowel (usually "ah") on both sides. This means a "V" sounds like "ahvah" and an "F" sounds like "ahfah" and so on. Most phonics books distinguish consonant sounds without such preceding vowel, but they do follow with a vowel in the form of the schwa. This is fine for most consonants, but the ones that are able to be maintained until breath is exhausted can be confusing with a schwa where they end a word. It's mostly ESL students who feel this confusion, but we think it doesn't hurt to teach those consonants without a schwa to native speakers as well, so where "V" sounds like "və" in most phonics books, in our book it is presented as "vvvvvvv" with no schwa. We apply this to all long consonant sounds in our audio files (L,M,N&R are also presented as long with a tiny schwa sound at the end though). If you have read this far, we take our hats off to you. Most would be fast asleep by now.

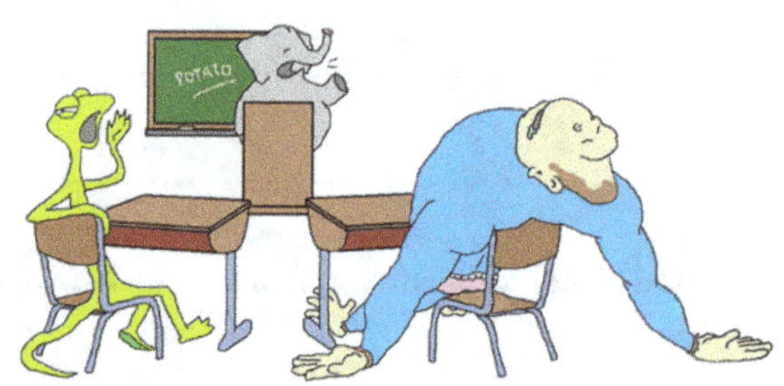

The next divergence is our use of Magic E. We chose Magic E for the fun potential. The Split Digraphs just can't seem to hold a crowd. Magic E is no longer used in most educational settings for many reasons, but mostly because as a rule it cannot be defined clearly. We do mention that split digraphs are better though, mainly to extend an olive branch to all the teachers we hope will buy our books.

And the final divergence we would like to mention is our choice of words. Our choice of words may seem a bit odd at times throughout the books, but we chose them for their potential for keeping kids engaged over their usefulness. We approach a phonics book as a tool to teach about sounds much more than vocabulary. Poop, vomit, spit, fart, snot, and burp are the most popular with our students. We tried to find a spot for booger, but alas...

Our word choice is also strange in that it includes words that have the long E vowel when teaching split digraphs. Most phonics books glance over the long E vowel. The argument we have heard for this is that it is difficult for the younger students, but we suspect that it's avoided more because it's difficult for authors to find suitable words. We decided to give it a try, and our experience is that the long E words we chose are not that difficult for our students to grasp. Given that English is their second language, we believe native English speaking kids will cope with them just fine. Also you may notice our sight words are not all actually sight words - oops! Anyway, we hope you enjoy our silly books.

Welcome students!

Hello. I am a gorilla. Together we are going to make a lot of very silly faces and sounds!

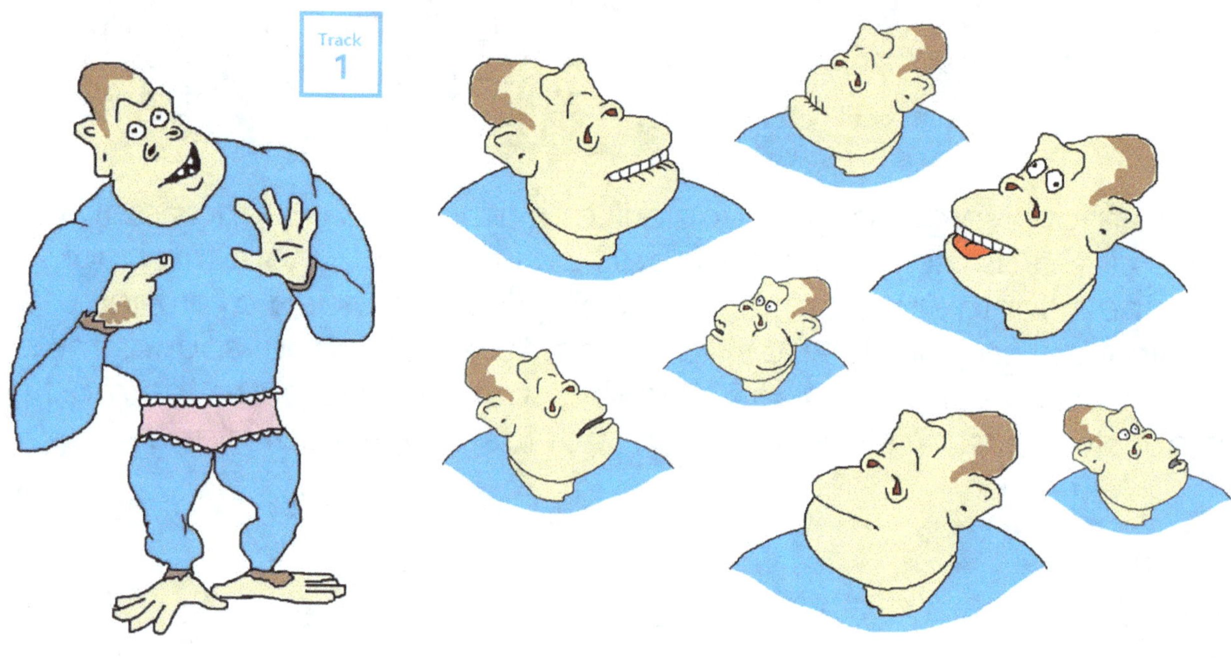

Hello. I am an elephant. I am a little wide. Some letters are also a little wide. You will see me around them!

Hello. I am a lizard. I am a little thin. Some letters are also a little thin. You will see me around them!

Hello. I am a mole. I like to dig! Some letters also like to dig. You will see me around them!

Hello. I am a pig. I don't care about letters. I just hang around.

I am a fly. I am smelly. You will see me around smelly stuff.

Let's get started...

Welcome Students!   5

Listen, point and say  

Tracks 0-9

Track 6

A B C D E

F G H I J

K L M N O

P Q R S T

U V W X Y

Z Z Z Z Z Z Z Z

Sing along:

A B C D E F G~
H I J K L M N ~
O P Q..

No, no!

It has to rhyme!

A B C D E F G ~
H I J K L-M-N-O-P ~
Q R S T U V ~
W X Y & Z

Listen, point, and make the sound  

Tracks 0-9

Track 8

A a　　B b　　C c

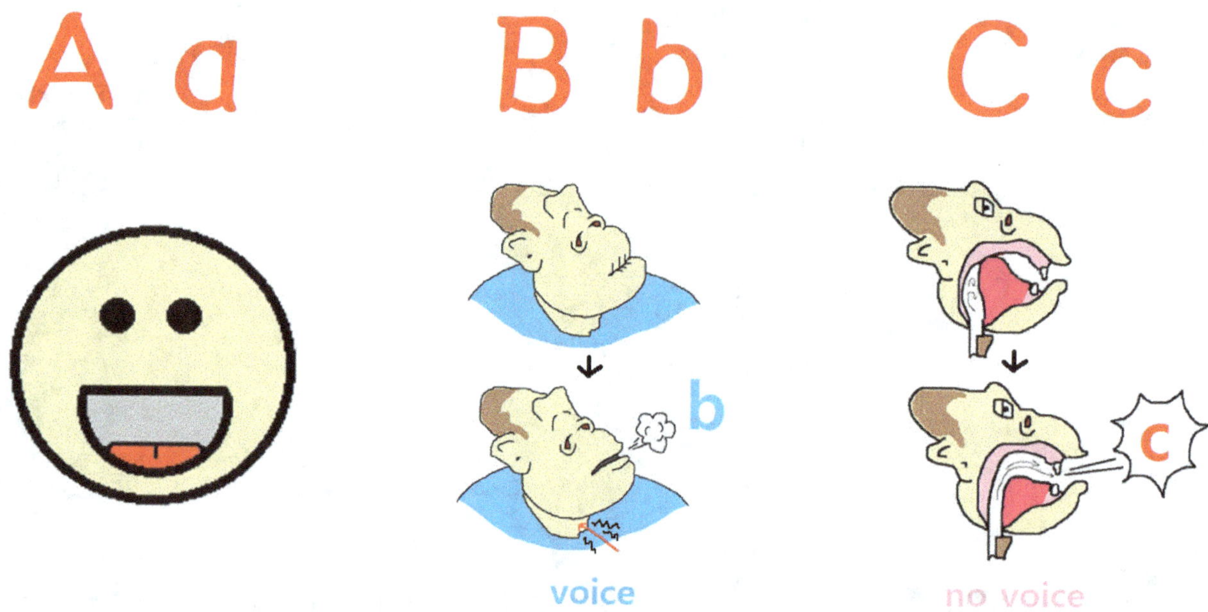

Listen and draw a line from the sound to the matching picture

Track 9

a　　b　　c

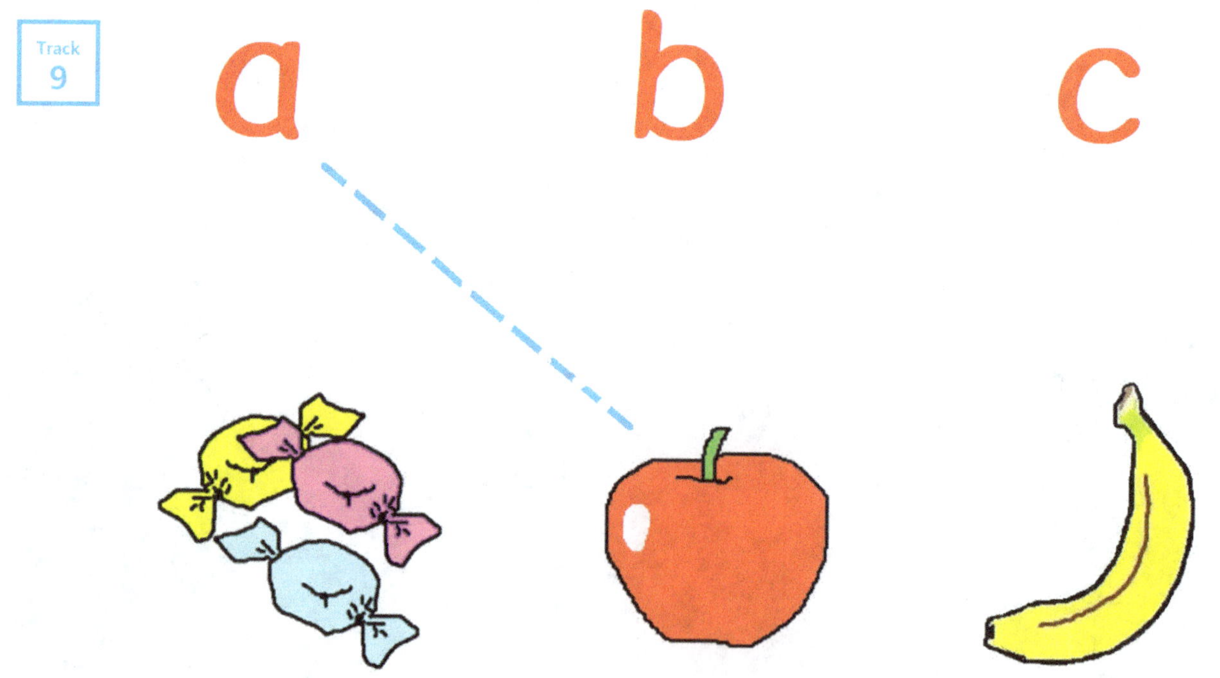

Follow the rules

A

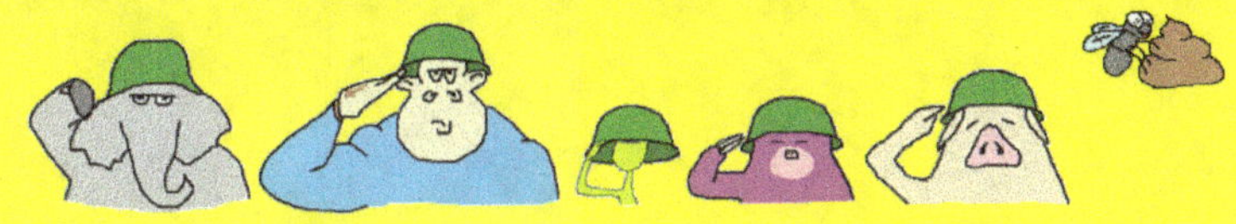

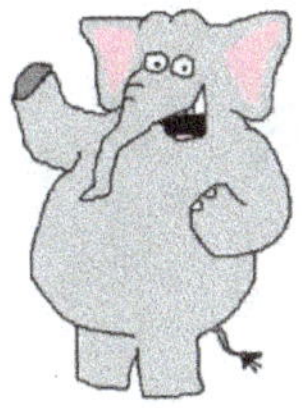

a

B

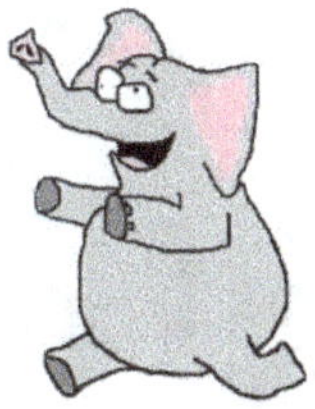

b

C

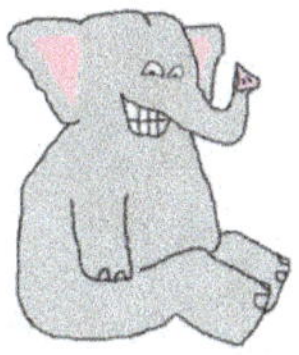

c

New Words

Tracks 10-19

Track
10

Aa

alligator angry ant apple

Bb

baby banana bird book

Cc

candy car cat cup

Do it again..and again.. and again!

Exercises

Writing practice

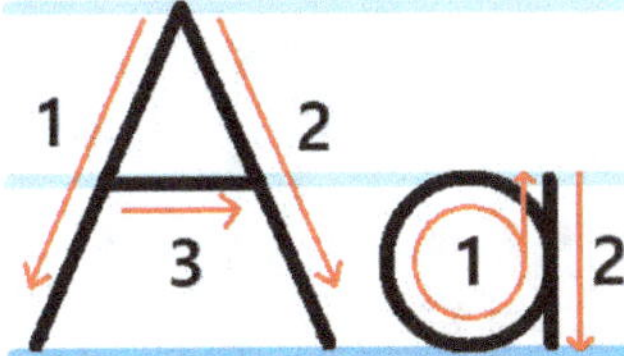

Word search

Listen and circle the word you hear

Exercises

Circle the word you hear

Track 12

Tracks 10-19

Write the matching letter

Chant

Track 13 

Sight words: a / an   and

An apple and a banana
An apple and a banana
An apple and a banana
And an angry cat

A cup and candy
A cup and candy
A cup and candy
And an angry bird

Circle the sound you hear

1. a   b   c   2. a   b   c

3. a   b   c   4. a   b   c

5. a   b   c   6. a   b   c

Listen and read along

Listen, point, and make the sound

Track 16

Tracks 10-19

D d   E e   F f

Listen and draw a line from the sound to the matching picture

Track 17

d   e   f

Follow the rules

D 1 D 2

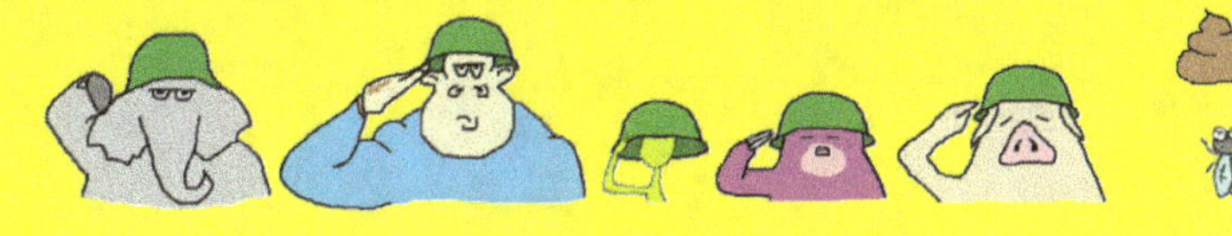

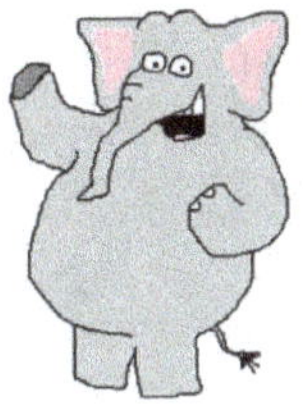

d 1 d 2

E 1 E 2 3 4

e e 2 1

F 1 F 2 3

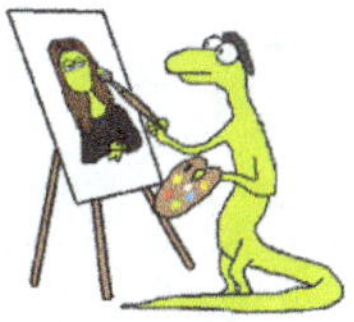

f 2 f 1

New Words

Listen, point and repeat the new words

Track 18

Do it again..and again.. and again!

Writing practice

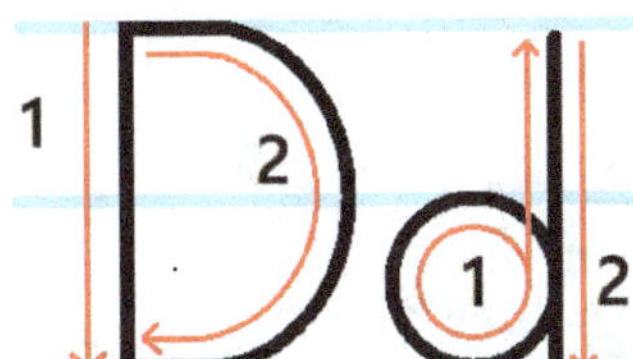
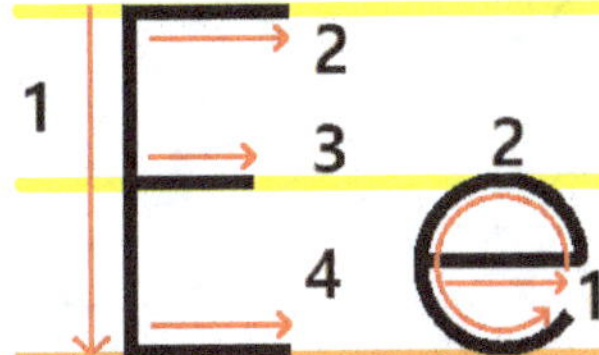
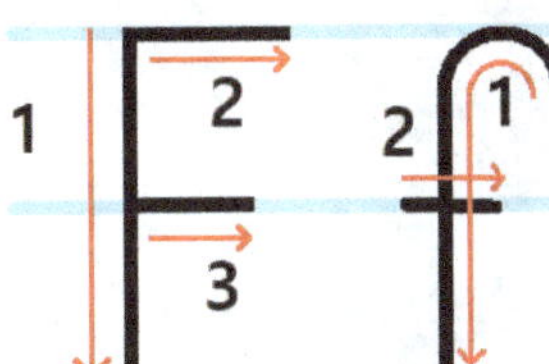

Word search   Listen and circle the word you hear

Track 19

Tracks 10-19

desk   **diamond**   **four**   **fish**   **flower**   **elephant**

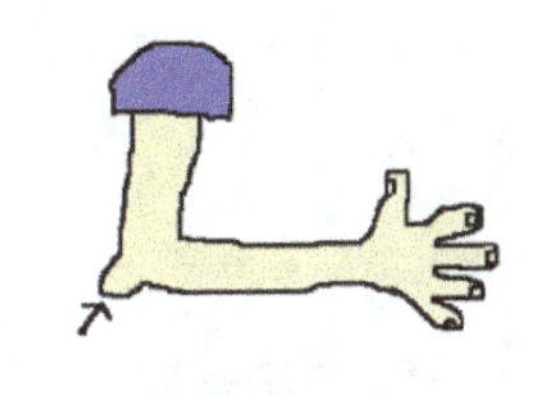     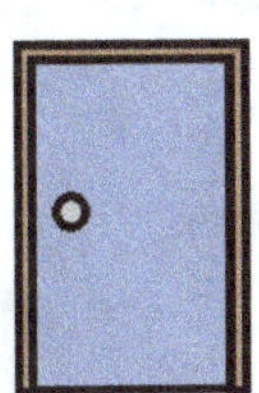 

elbow   **elf**   **dog**   **frog**   **door**   **egg**

Exercises

Circle the word you hear

Tracks 20-29

Track 20

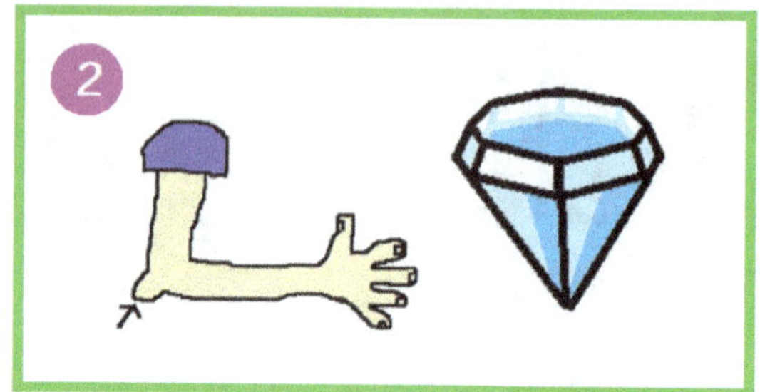
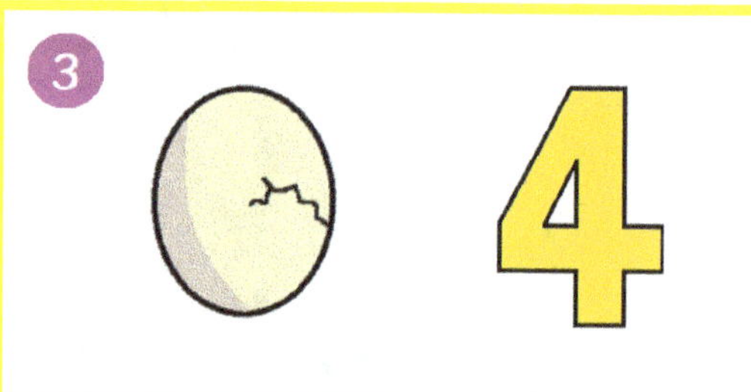

Write the matching letter

____

____

Chant

Track 21

New sight words: all on

A fish and a frog
And an elephant elbow
All on a diamond desk

A book and a cup
And an angry ant
All on a diamond desk

Story

Circle the sound you hear

1. d e f
2. d e f
3. d e f
4. d e f
5. d e f
6. d e f

Listen and read along

New sight words: in   the

Flowers

An egg in the flowers.

A bird in the egg?

A dog!   A dog egg?!

Listen, point, and make the sound

Track 24

Tracks 20-29

G g   H h   I i

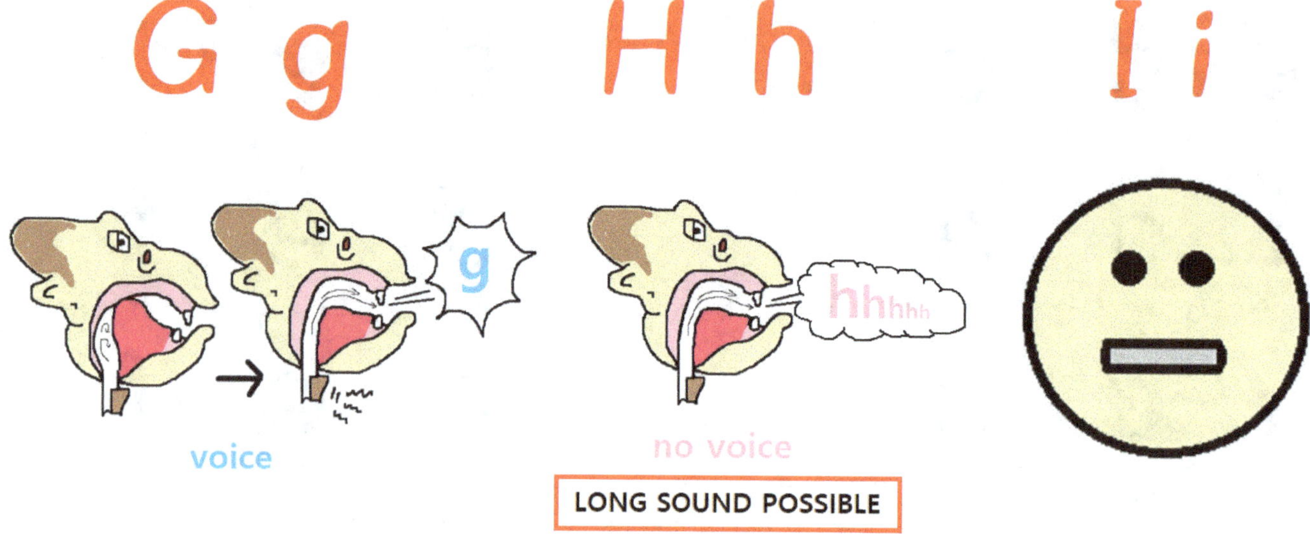

Listen and draw a line from the sound to the matching picture

Track 25

g   h   i

Follow the rules

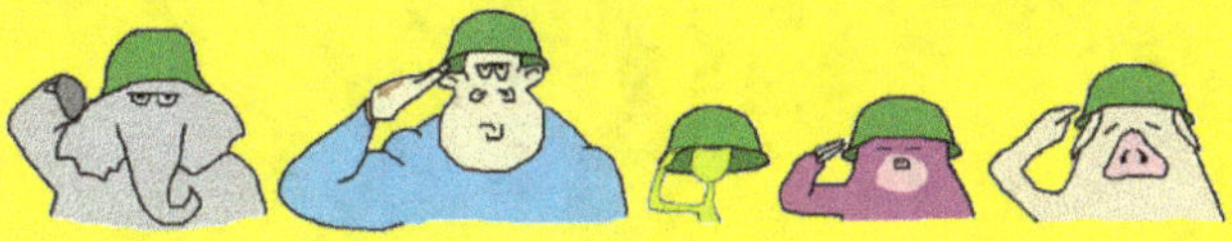

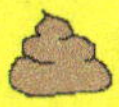

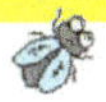

G G

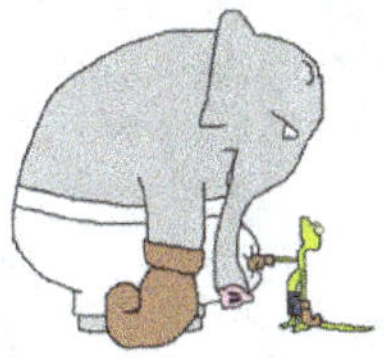

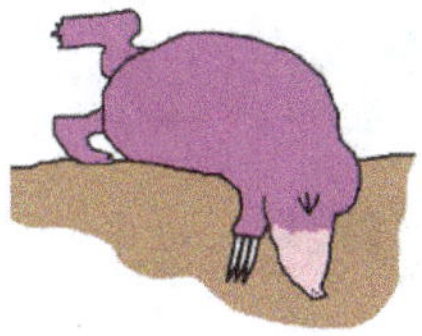

g g

H H

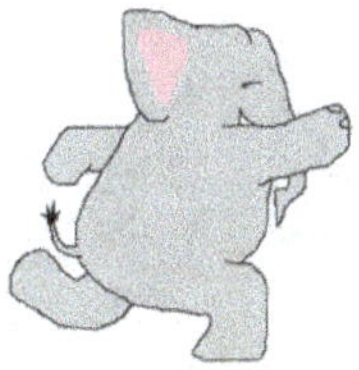

h h

I I

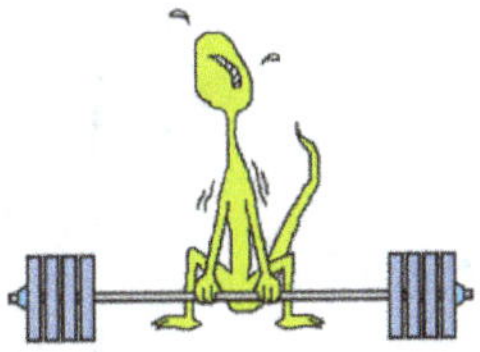

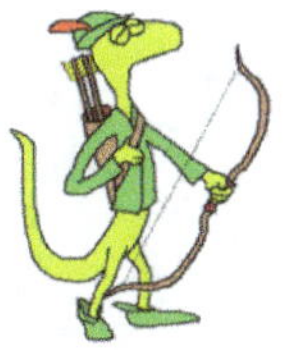

i i

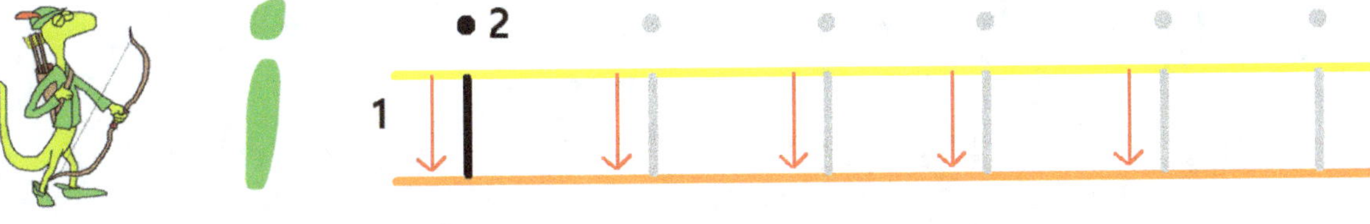

New Words

Listen, point and repeat the new words

Track 26

Gg

gold   good   gorilla   grass

Hh

happy   hat   hill   house

Ii

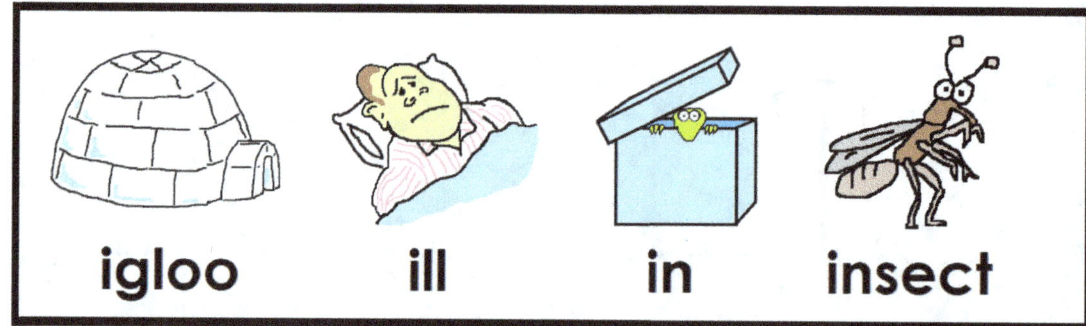

igloo   ill   in   insect

Do it again..and again.. and again!

Exercises

Writing practice

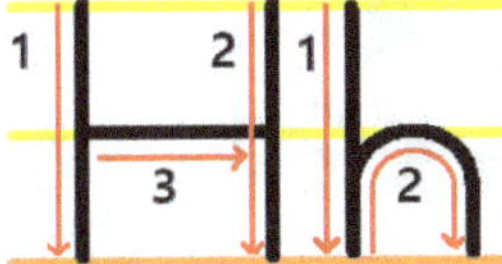

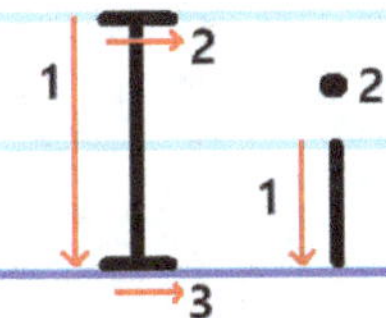

Word search

Listen and circle the word you hear

Tracks 20-29

Exercises

Circle the word you hear

Track 28

Tracks 20-29

Write the matching letter

Chant

Track 29

Ill in a hat
Ill in a good hat
Ill in a good gold hat

Ill in a house
Ill in a good house
Ill in a good gold house

Circle the sound you hear

Track 30

Tracks 30-39

1	g	h	i	**2**	g	h	i
3	g	h	i	**4**	g	h	i
5	g	h	i	**6**	g	h	i

Listen and read along

Track 31

New sight words: no

Grass on a hill.

A happy insect in the grass.

A happy gorilla on a hill.

No happy insect in the grass.

UNIT 4 Single-Letter Sounds

Listen, point, and make the sound

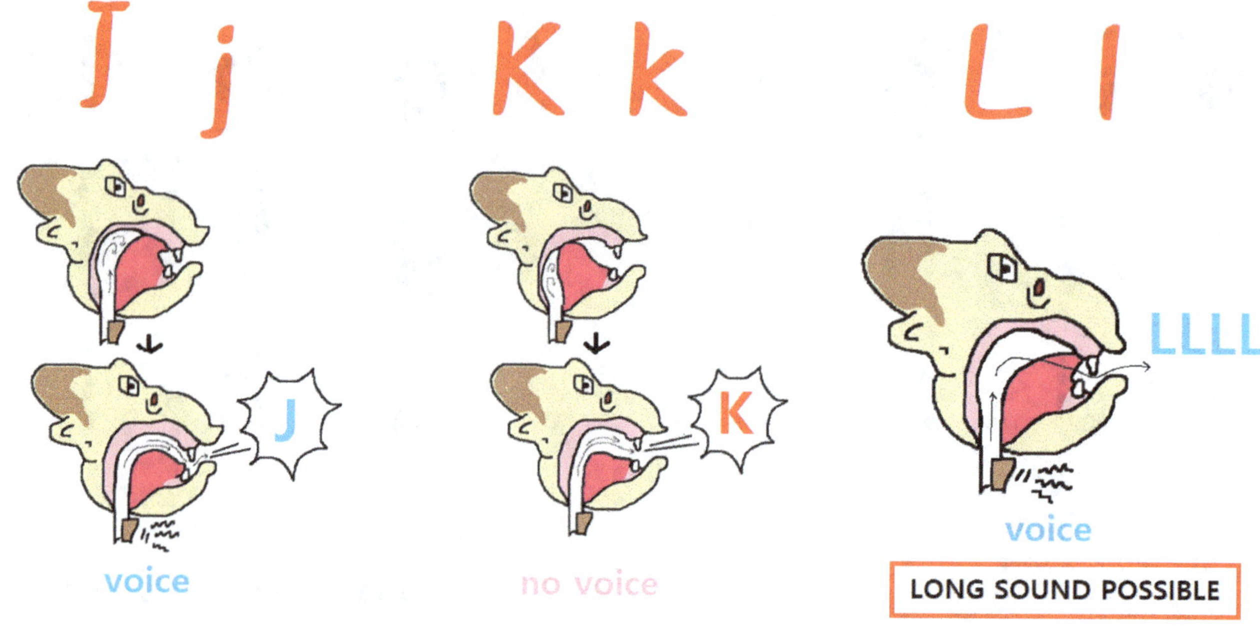

Listen and draw a line from the sound to the matching picture

Follow the rules

New Words

Listen, point and repeat the new words

Jj

jail   jam   jet   jump

Kk

kangaroo   key   kick   kite

Ll

leg   lemon   lid   lion

Do it again..and again.. and again!

Writing practice

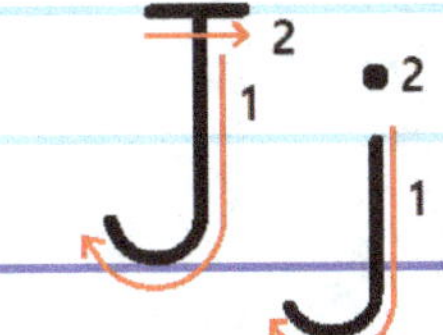

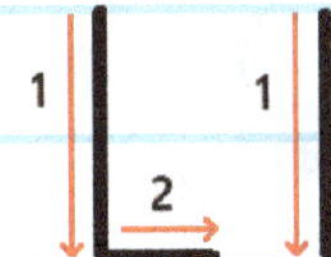

Word search   *Listen and circle the word you hear*   Track 35

Tracks 30-39

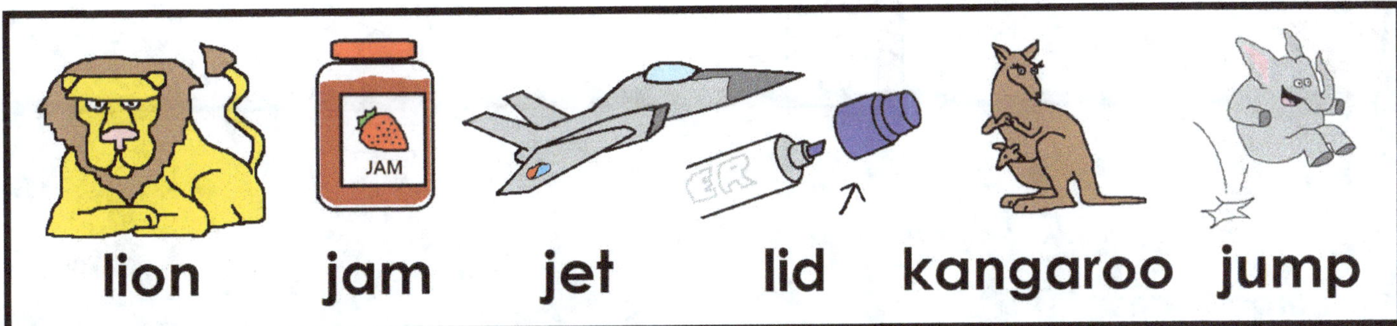

lion   **jam**   **jet**   **lid**   **kangaroo**   **jump**

leg   **kite**   **jail**   **lemon**   **key**   **kick**

Exercises

Circle the word you hear

Tracks 30-39

Track 36

Write the matching letter

Chant

Track 37

New sight words: lift   like

Lemon jam
Lemon jam
Lift the lid
Kangaroos like lemon jam

Kangaroo jam
Kangaroo jam
Lift the lid
Lions like kangaroo jam

Story

Circle the sound you hear

1. j k l   2. j k l

3. j k l   4. j k l

5. j k l   6. j k l

Listen and read along

New sight words: get

Lion and kangaroo in jail.

Kick the leg! Get the key!

Jump in the jet!

Lion in jail.

Review

Listen, point, and say

Track 40

Tracks 40-49

A a 

B b 

C c 

D d 

E e 

F f 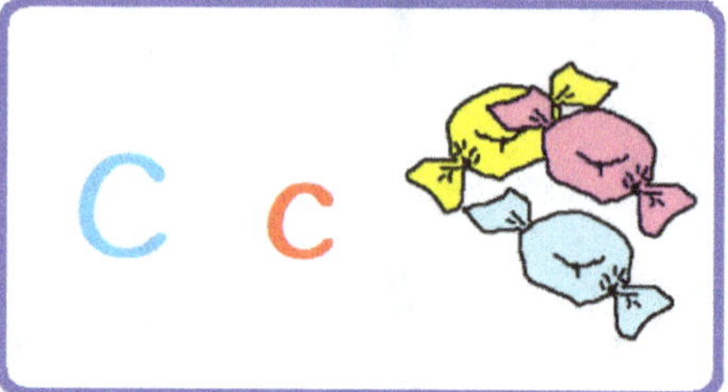

G g 

H h 

I i 

J j 

K k 

L l 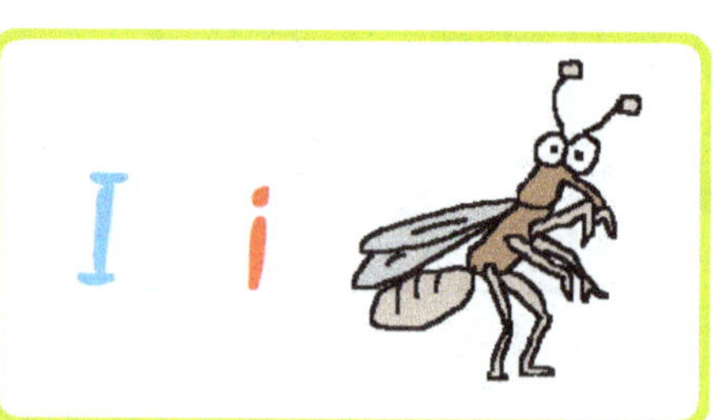

Review

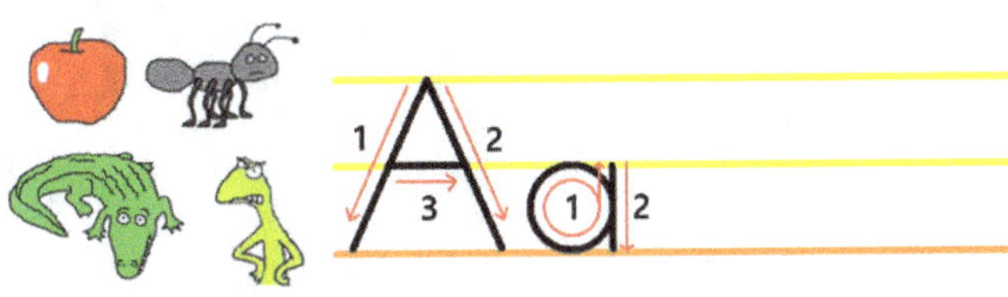 Aa

 Bb

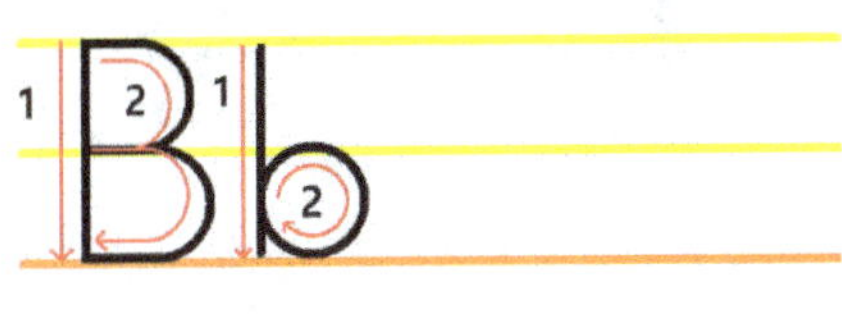 Cc

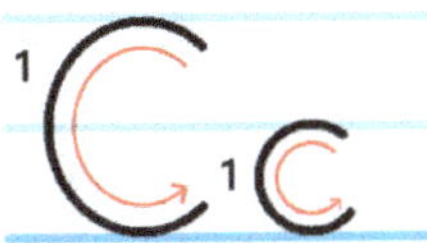 Dd

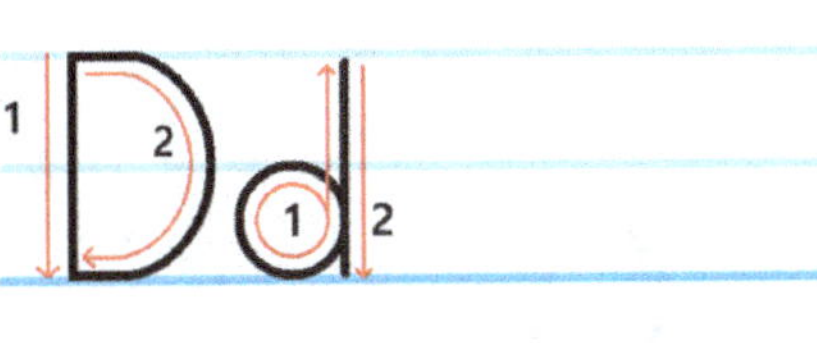 Ee

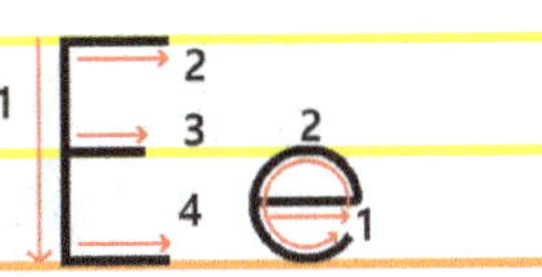 Ff

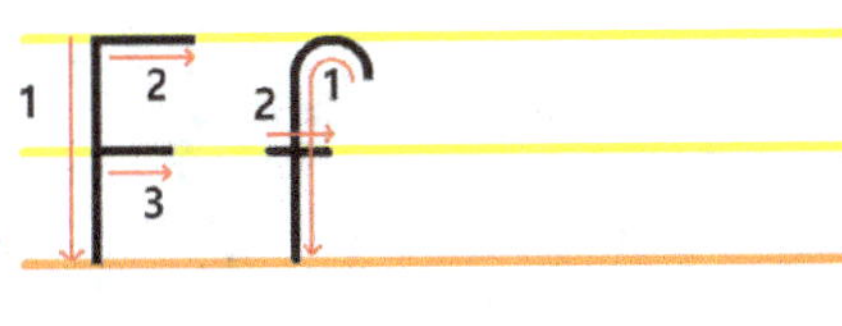 Gg

 Hh

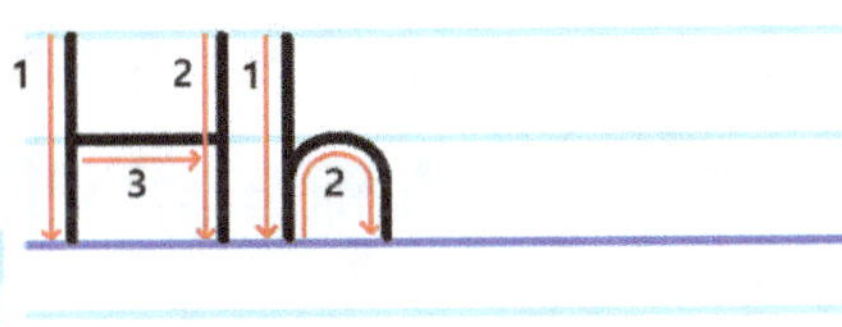 Ii

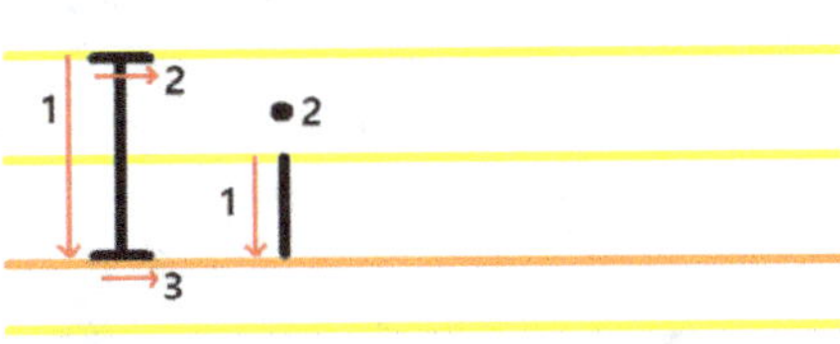 Jj

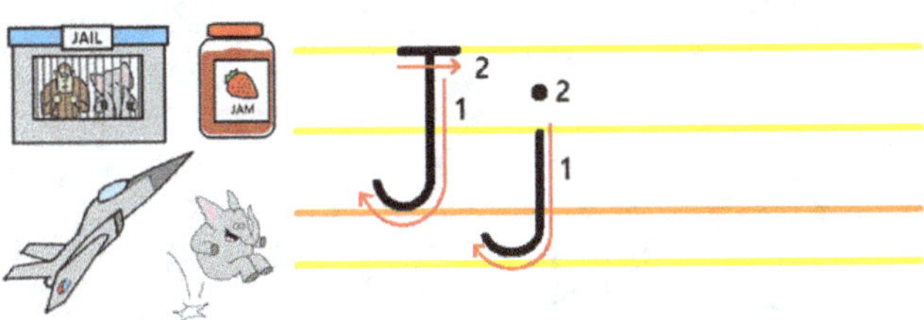 Kk

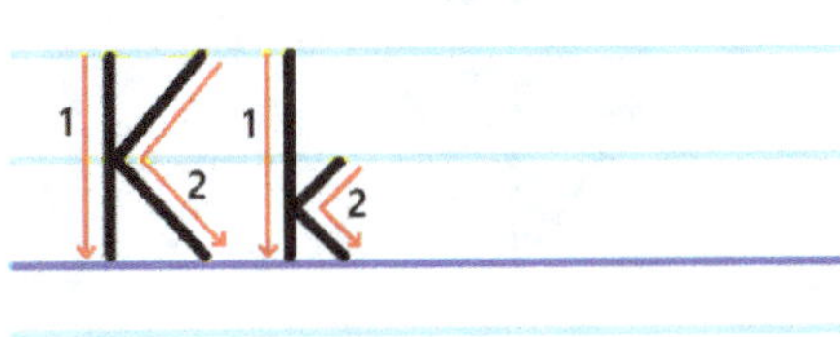 Ll

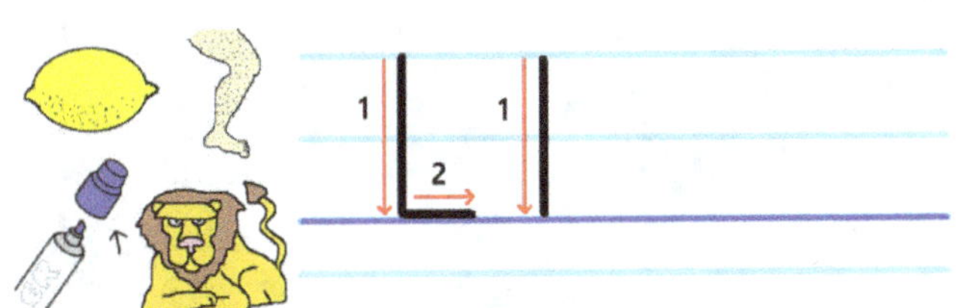

Review

Find the path

1. H   a
2. A   h
3. G   d
4. D   g

Listen and circle the matching letter

Tracks 40-49

1	4 d e f	2	 i h j
3	i g k	4	j k l
5	a c f	6	d h b

Listen and circle. Then write the word

Track 42

Tracks 40-49

1   elf

2    egg

3    kick

4    jail

5    gold

UNIT 5   Single-Letter Sounds

Listen, point, and make the sound

Track 43

Tracks 40-49

M m   N n   O o

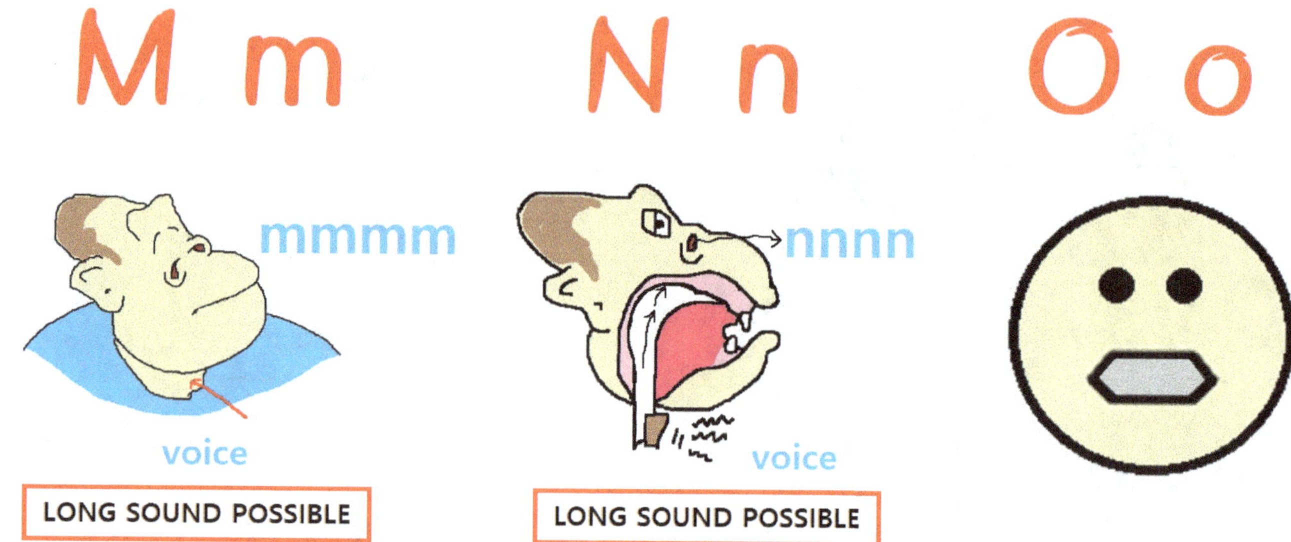

Listen and draw a line from the sound to the matching picture

Track 44

m   n   o

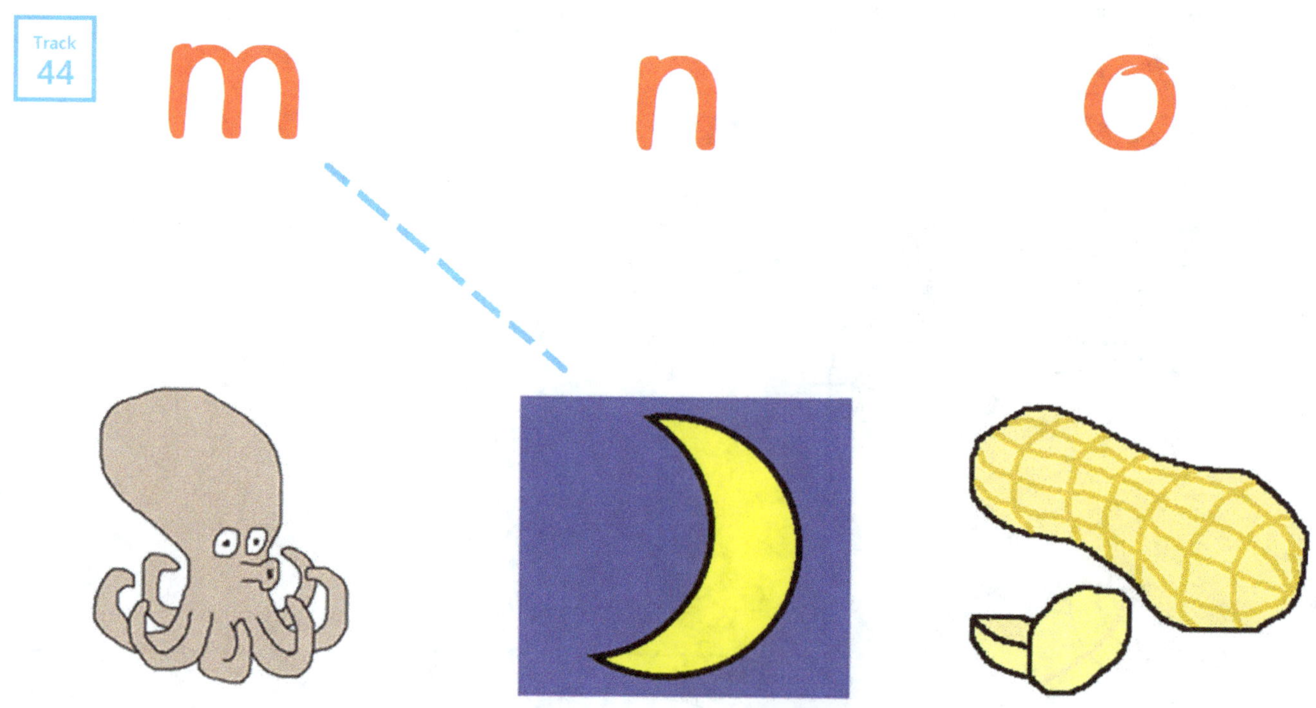

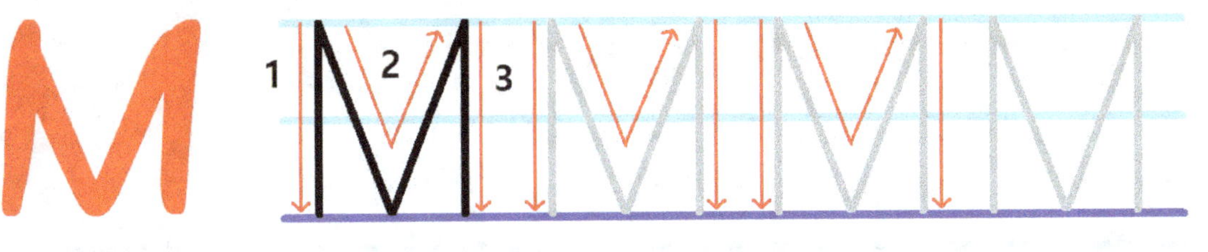

M

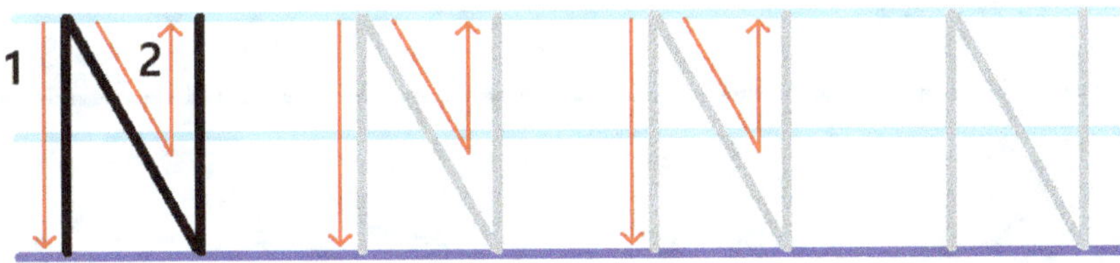

m

N

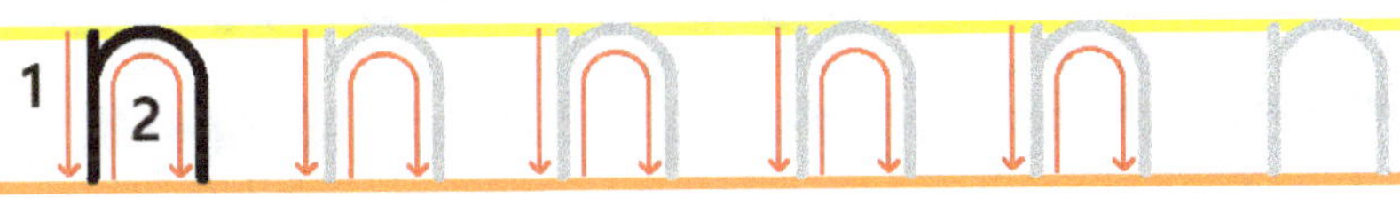

n

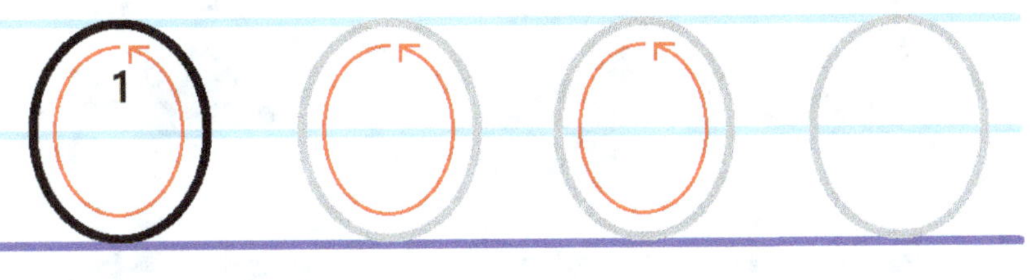

O

o

Tracks 40-49

Mm

| milk | monkey | moon | mouse |

Nn

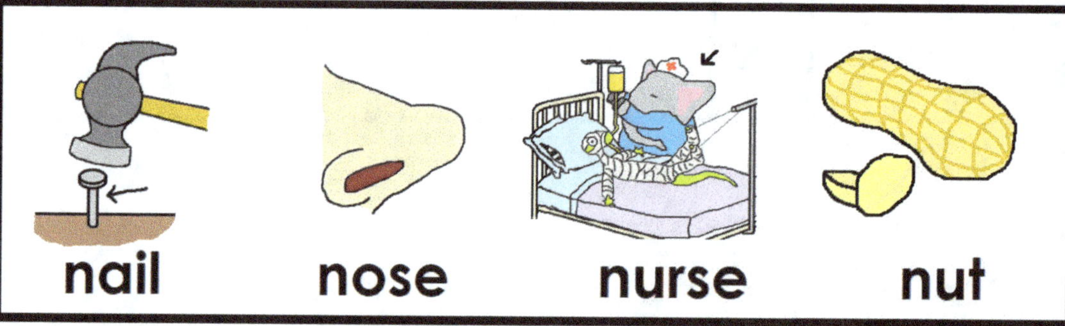

| nail | nose | nurse | nut |

Oo

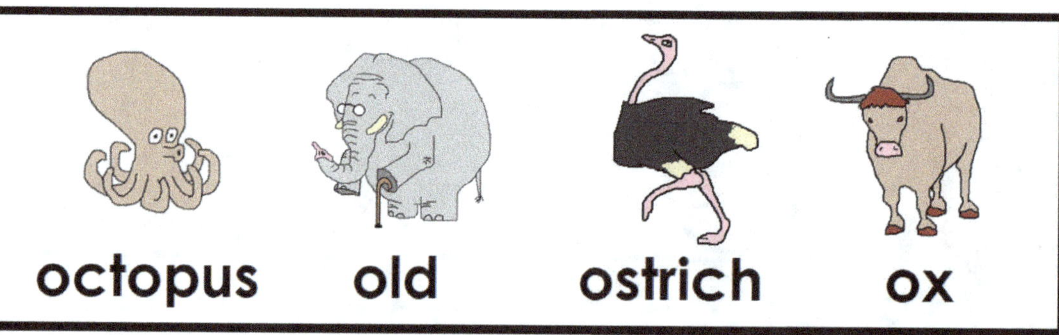

| octopus | old | ostrich | ox |

Do it again..and again.. and again!

Exercises

Writing practice

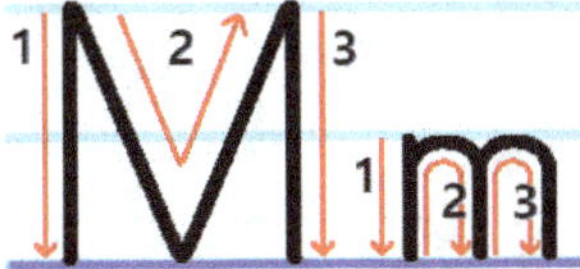

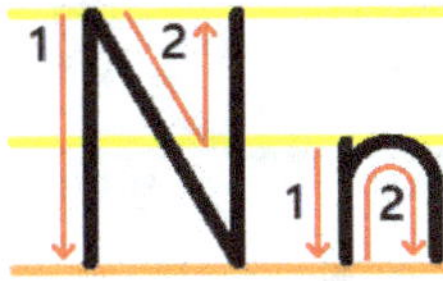

Word search
Listen and circle the word you hear

Tracks 40-49

octopus   **milk**   **ox**   **ostrich**   **nut**   **monkey**

  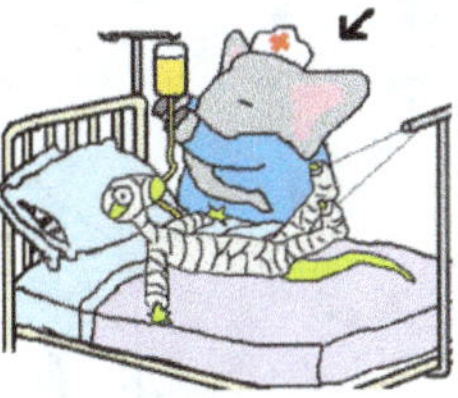  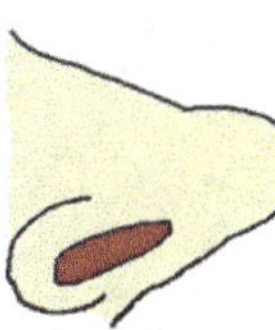 

nail   **old**   **nurse**   **moon**   **nose**   **mouse**

Exercises

Circle the word you hear

Track 47

Tracks 40-49

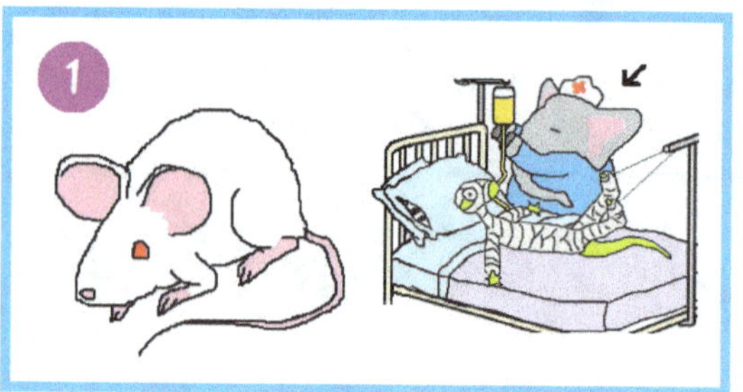

Write the matching letter

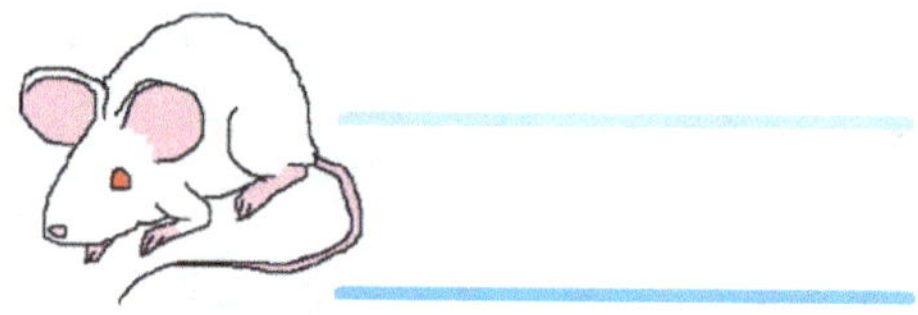

Chant

New sight words: oh not

Old monkey milk
And an octopus nose

Old monkey milk
And an octopus nose

Oh no! Oh no!
Not old monkey millk!

Track 48

Circle the sound you hear

Tracks 40-49

1. m n o   2. m n o

3. m n o   4. m n o

5. m n o   6. m n o

Listen and read along

Ox and mouse and ostrich on the moon.

A nail!   Get the nail!

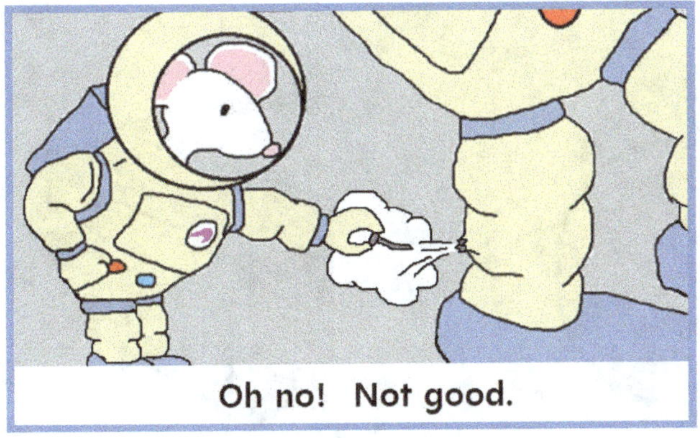
Oh no! Not good.

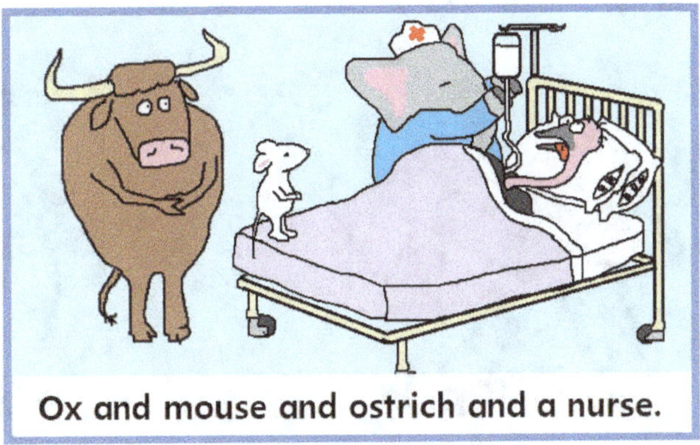
Ox and mouse and ostrich and a nurse.

Listen, point, and make the sound

Track 51

Tracks 50-59

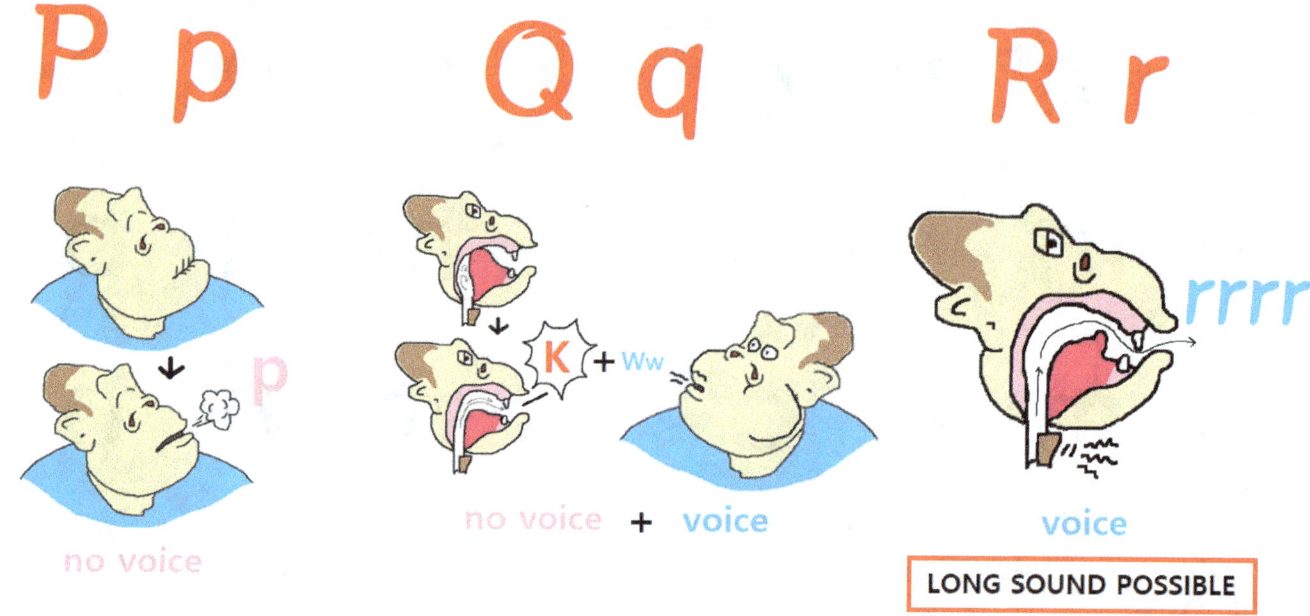

Listen and draw a line from the sound to the matching picture

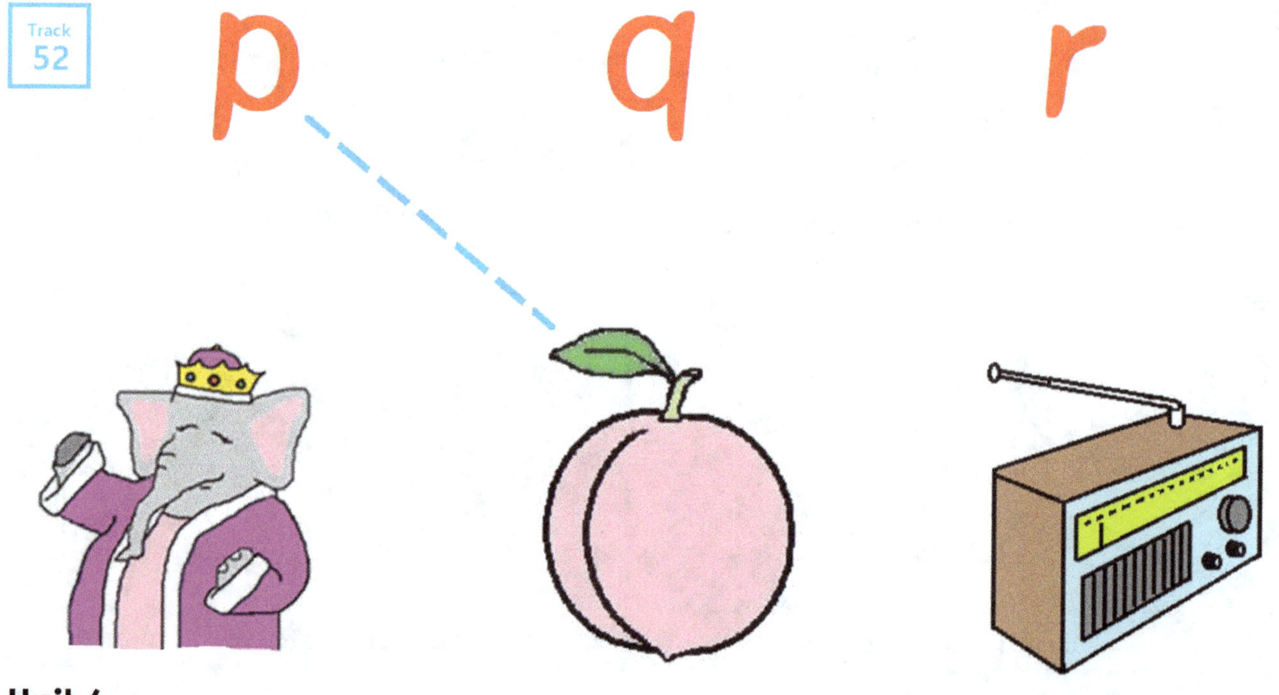

Follow the rules

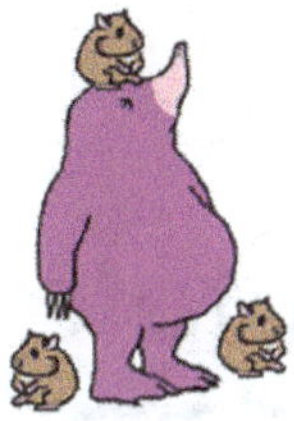

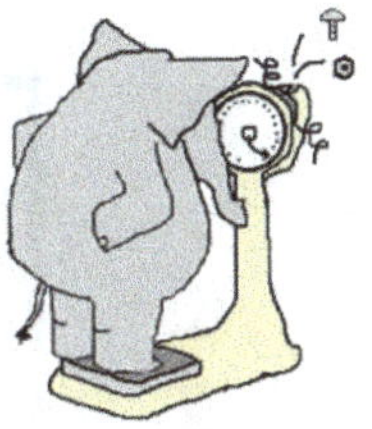

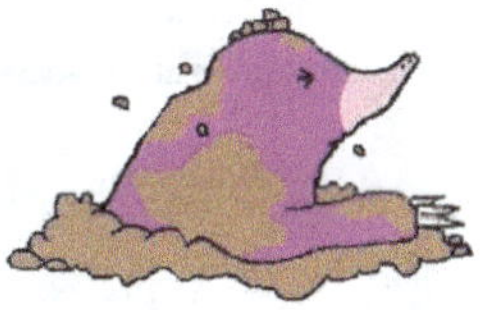

P p

Q q

R r

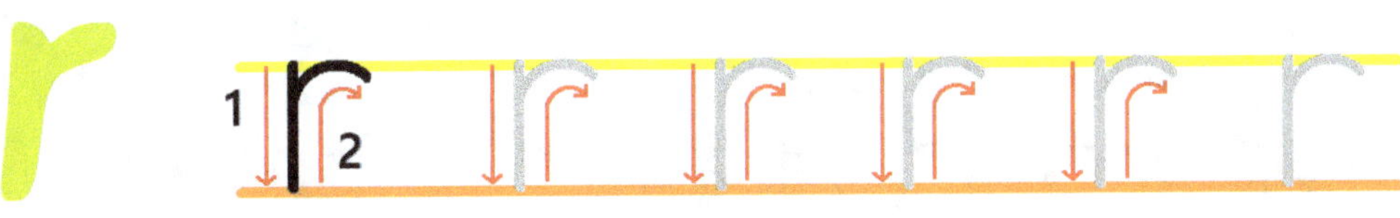

New Words

Listen, point and repeat the new words

Track 53

Pp

pants   peach   poop   potato

Qq

queen   question   quick   quiet

Rr

radio   red   robot   run

Do it again.. and again.. and again!

Exercises

Writing practice

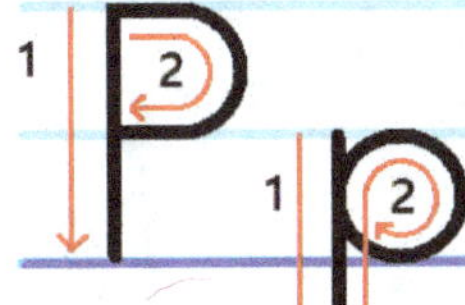

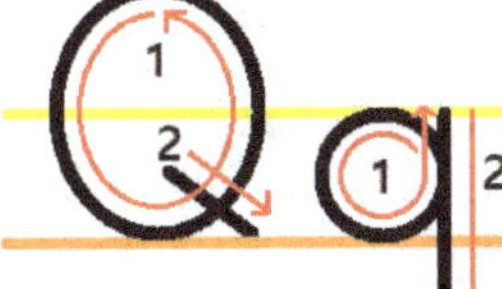

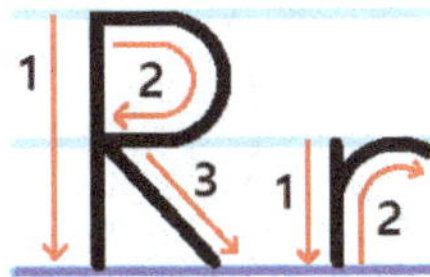

Word search *Listen and circle the word you hear*

Tracks 50-59

Exercises

Circle the word you hear

Track 55

Tracks 50-59

1

2

3

4

Write the matching letter

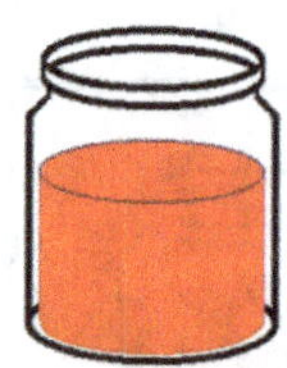

Chant

Track 56

New sight words: did you your

A quick quiet question:

Did you poop your pants?

A quick quiet question:

Did you poop your pants?

Story

Circle the sound you hear

1. p q r   2. p q r

3. p q r   4. p q r

5. p q r   6. p q r

Listen and read along

New sight words: has   put

Listen, point, and make the sound

Tracks 50-59

S s   T t   U u   V v

Listen and draw a line from the sound to the matching picture

s   t   u   v

S s

S s

T

t 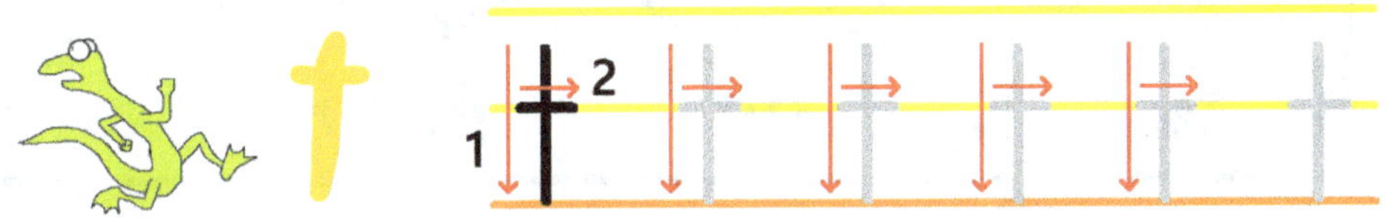

U

u

V

v 

New Words

Listen, point and repeat the new words

Ss

sad   sit   smell   sun

Tt

tear   ten   tiger   time

Uu

umbrella   umpire   under   up

Vv

van   vest   violin   vomit

Do it again..and again.. and again!

Exercises

Writing practice

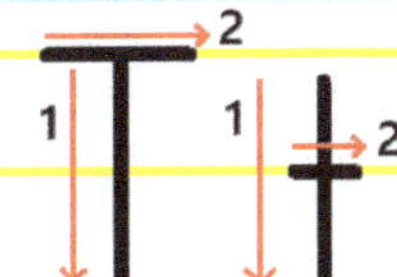

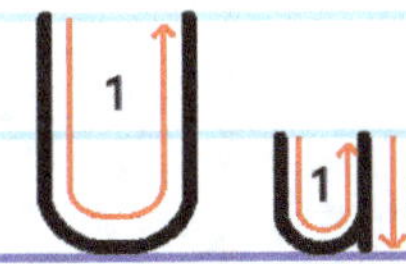

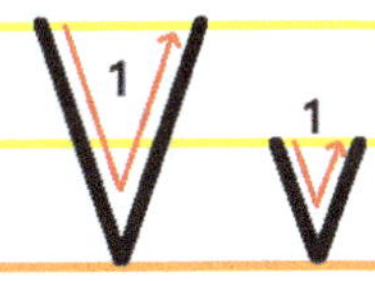

Word search Listen and circle the word you hear

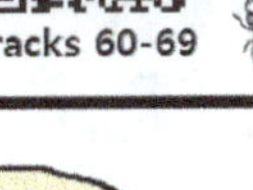

Tracks 60-69

| sad | under | up | ten | vest | van | smell | tear |

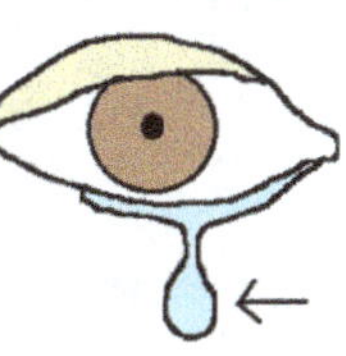

| sit | time | sun | umbrella | tiger | vomit | violin | umpire |

Exercises

Circle the word you hear

Track **63**

Tracks 60-69

Write the matching letter

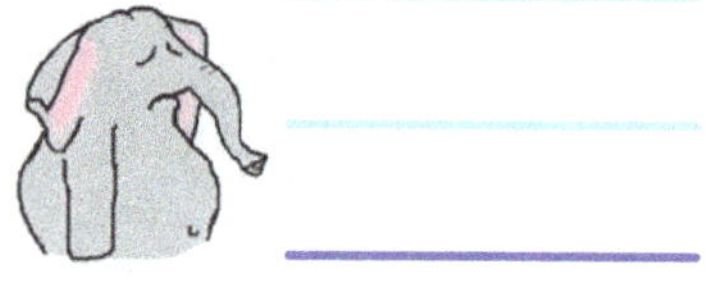

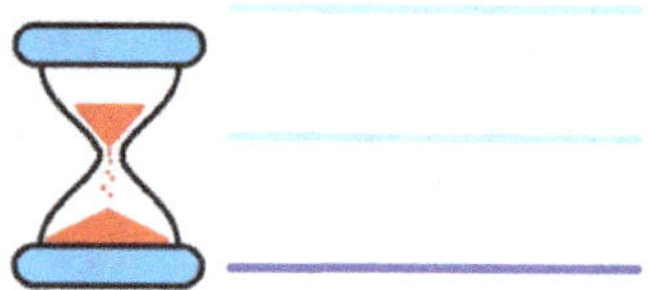
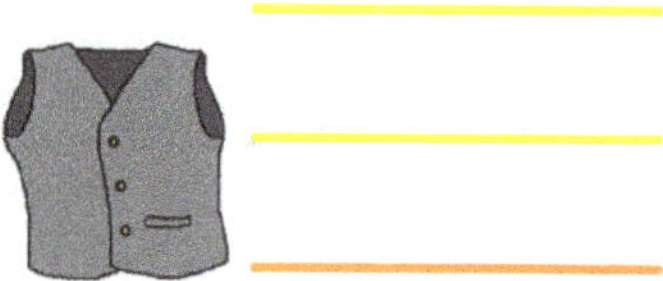

Chant

Track **64**

New words: one   by   fella (fellow)

Sad tiger sits
Under the sun,
Tiger tears, tiger tears,
One by one.

Sad tiger sits
Under an umbrella,
Violins! Violins!
Sad, sad fella.

Circle the sound you hear

Track 65

Tracks 60-69

1. s t u v
2. s t u v
3. s t u v
4. s t u v
5. s t u v
6. s t u v

Listen and read along

Track 66

New sight words: says go to win

Listen, point, and make the sound

Track 67

Tracks 60-69

W w   X x   Y y   Z z

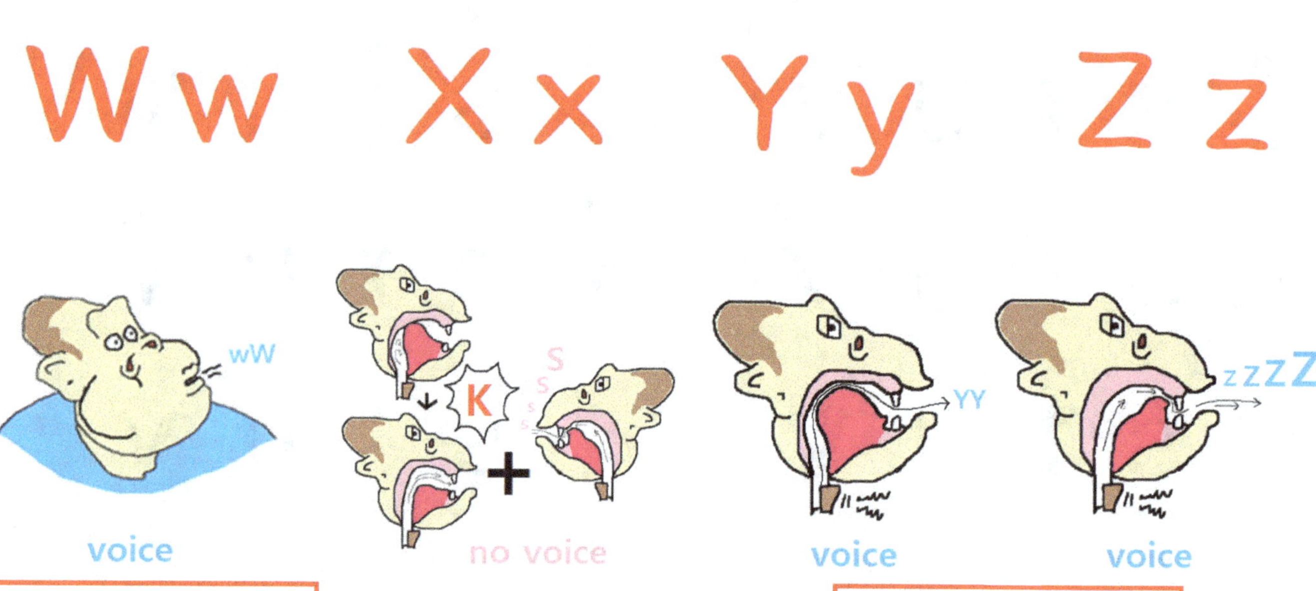

Listen and draw a line from the sound to the matching picture

w   x   y   z

Track 68

W w

W  w

X x

X x

Y y

Y y

Z z

Z z

New Words

Listen, point and repeat the new words

Tracks 60-69

Ww

| water | wave | window | wish |

Xx

| box | fix | fox | six |

Yy

| yawn | yellow | young | yo-yo |

Zz

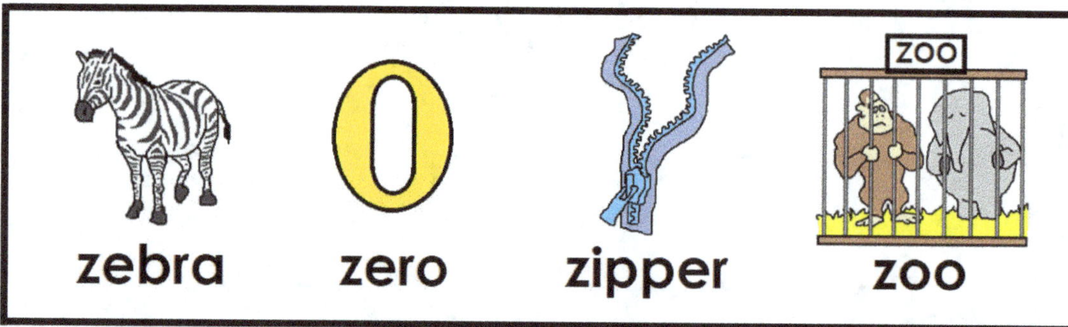

| zebra | zero | zipper | zoo |

Do it again..and again.. and again!

Exercises

Writing practice

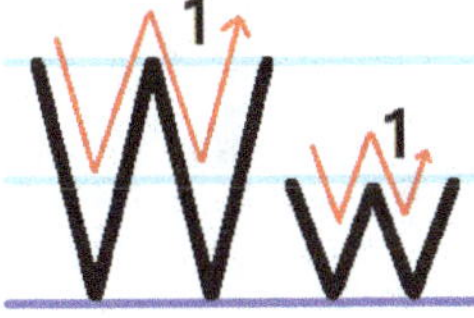

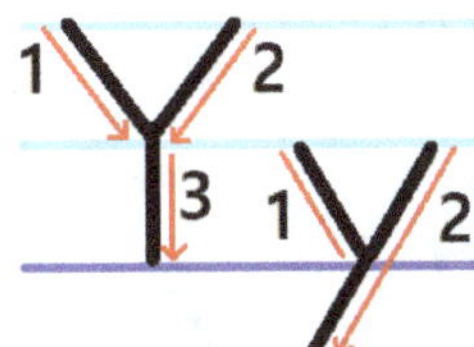

Word search   Listen and circle the word you hear

Track 70

Tracks 70-79

window   zero   young   wave   yellow   zipper   yo-yo   box

fix   zebra   zoo   water   fox   yawn   six   wish

Exercises

Circle the word you hear

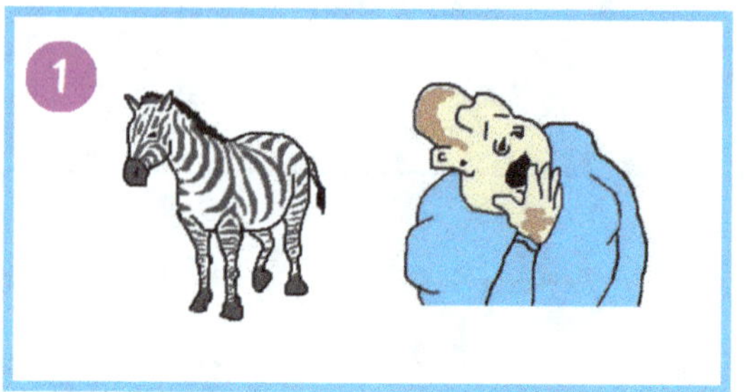

Write the matching letter

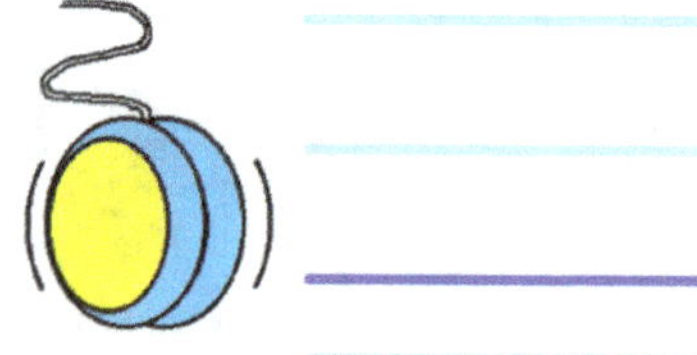

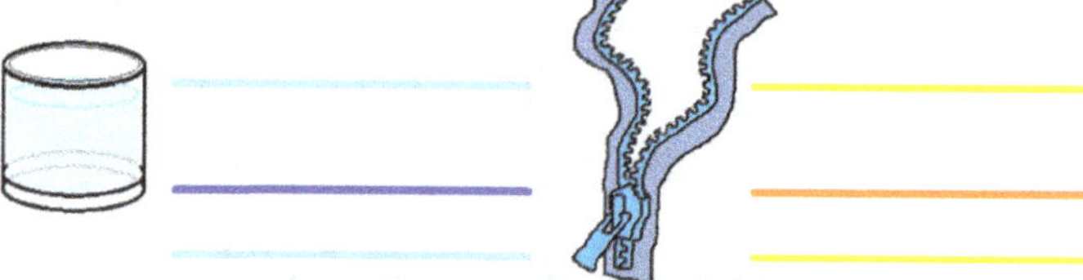

Chant

I wish I had a zebra,

I wish I had a fox,

I wish I had a yo yo,

All in a yellow box,

I wish I did,

I wish I did,

I wish it had a yellow lid!

New sight words: I   had   it

Story

Circle the sound you hear

Tracks 70-79

1. w x y z
2. w x y z
3. w x y z
4. w x y z
5. w x y z
6. w x y z

Listen and read along

New sight words: wait

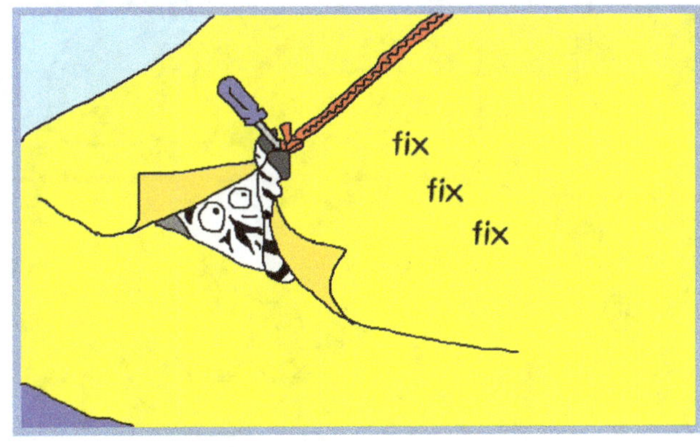

Review

Listen, point, and say

Tracks 70-79

M m 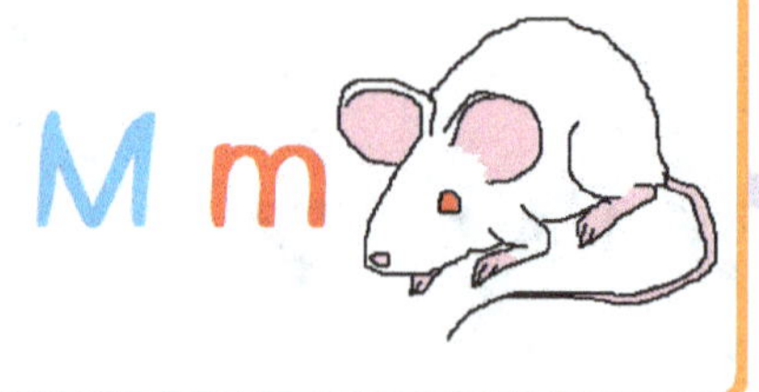

N n 

O o 

P p 

Q q 

R r 

S s 

T t 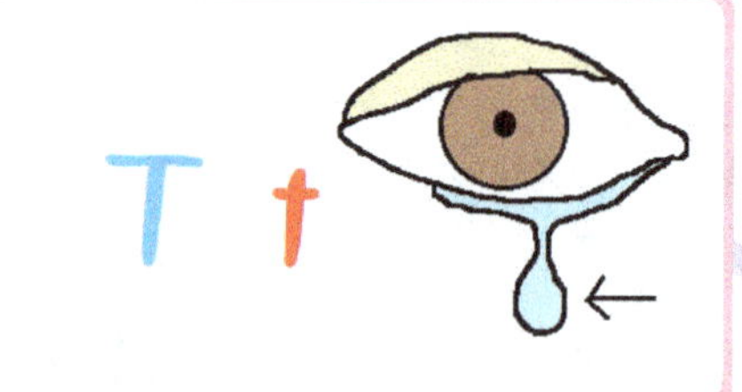

U u 

V v 

W w 

X x 

Y y 

Z z 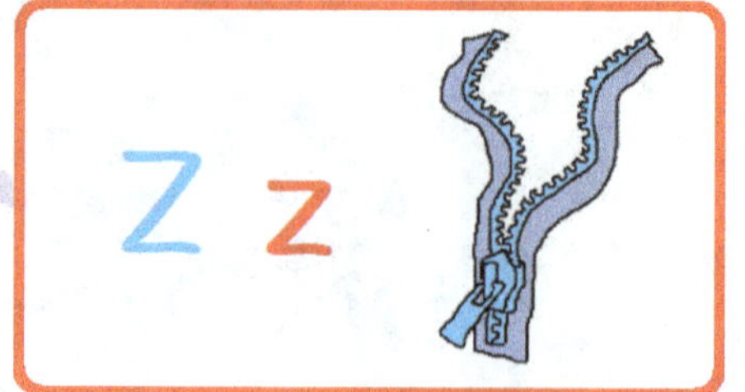

Review

Say all the words and write the letter

  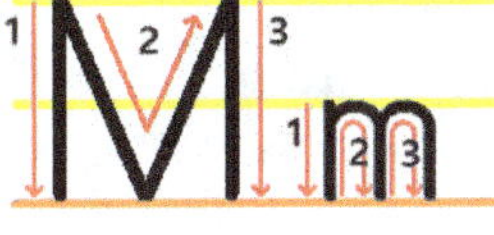
M m

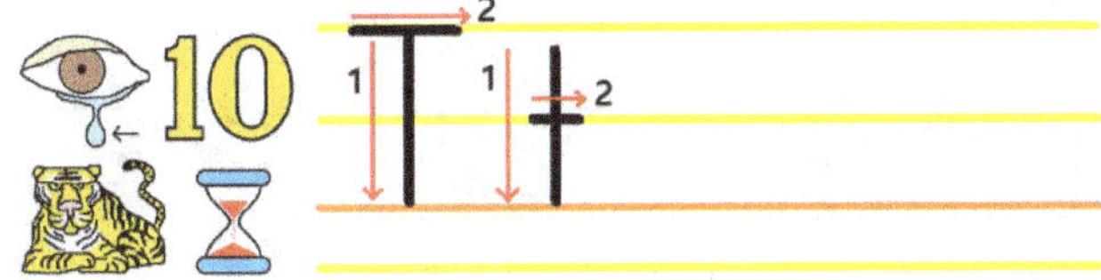
T t

N n

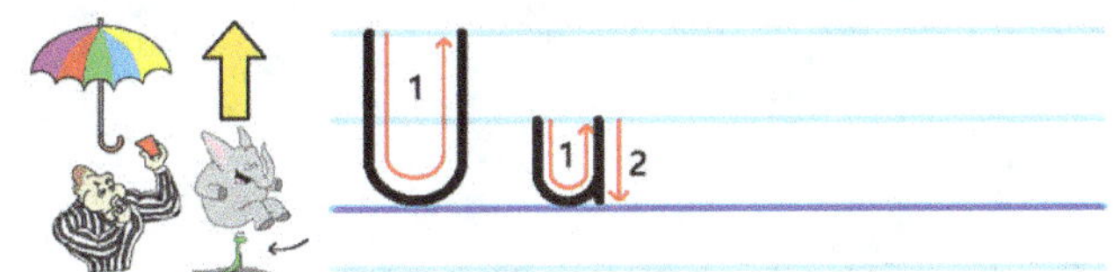
U u

O o

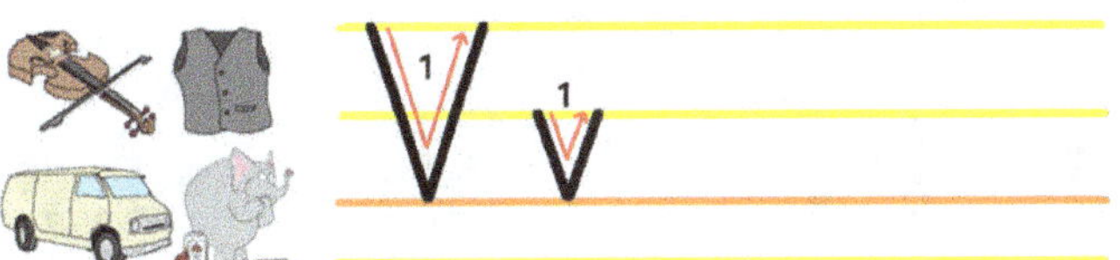
V v

P p

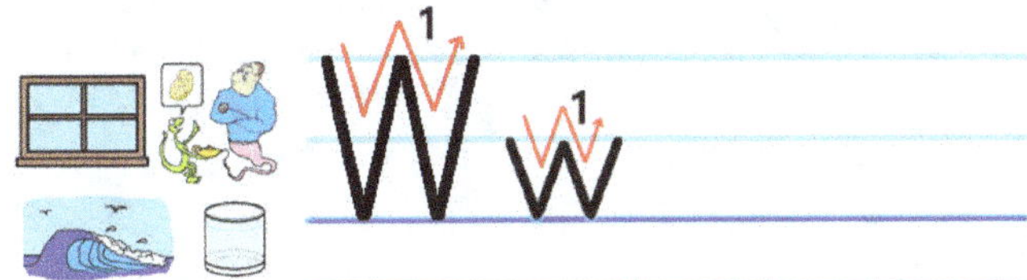
W w

 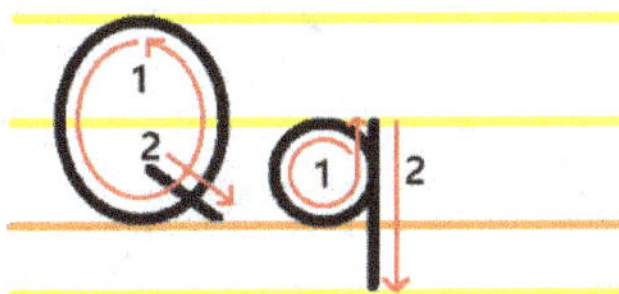
Q q

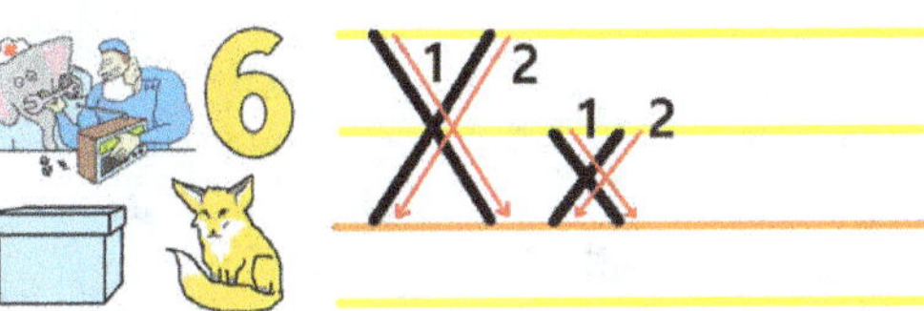
X x

 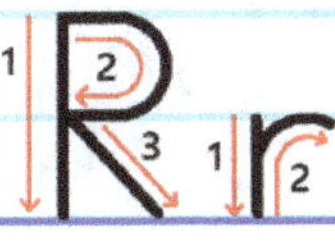
R r

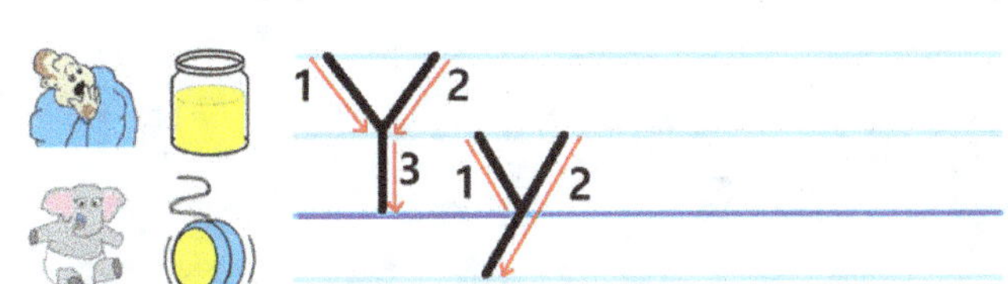
Y y

S s

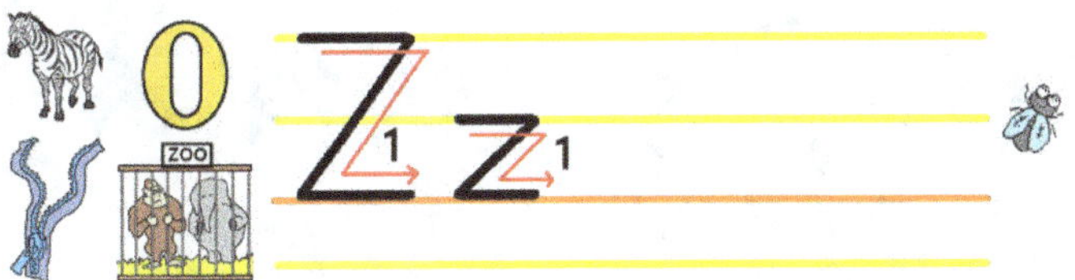
Z z

Review

Find the path

1	**M**					**r**
2	**R**					**t**
3	**T**					**m**
4	**U**					**y**
5	**Y**	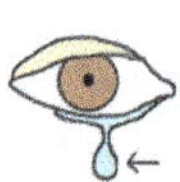				**u**

Listen and circle the matching letter

Track 76

Tracks 70-79

1		m s v	2		p s z
3	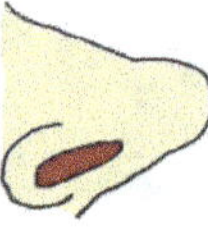	r n t	4		y u w
5		o q x	6		m t p

Review

Write the word twice

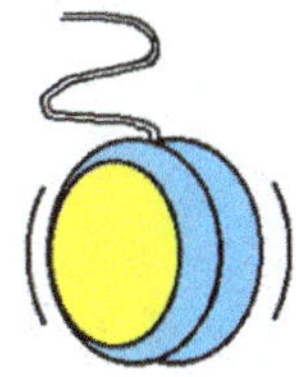

1   yo-yo

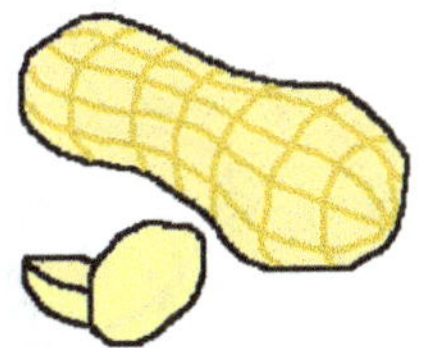

2   nut

3   wave

4   time

5   mouse

Review

Listen, find, and circle

Tracks 70-79

1 **b**ird   2 **e**gg   3 **r**un

4 **c**andy   5 **m**ilk   6 **z**ebra

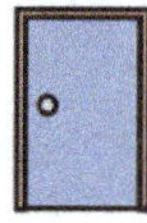     

Review

Find the wrong ones and cross them out
(Say the first letter of each word... is it right?)

1   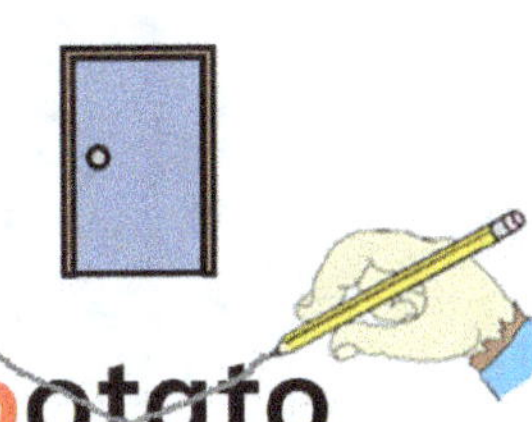 

cup   six   potato   four   leg

2     

wave   gorilla   kick   house   kite

3     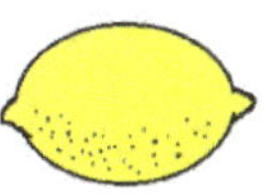

jump   poop   fox   kangaroo   lemon

4     

mouse   queen   banana   lion   in

Test

Listen and circle the word you hear a  Track 78 b  Track 79 c  Track 80

1       

2      

3      

4     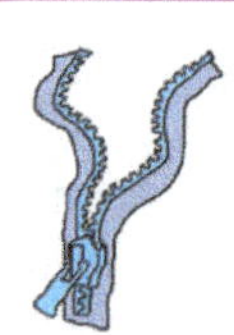 

5   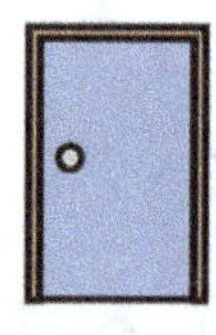   

Test  

Listen and write the sound you hear a  b  c 

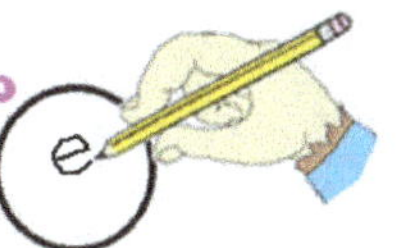

Tracks 80-87

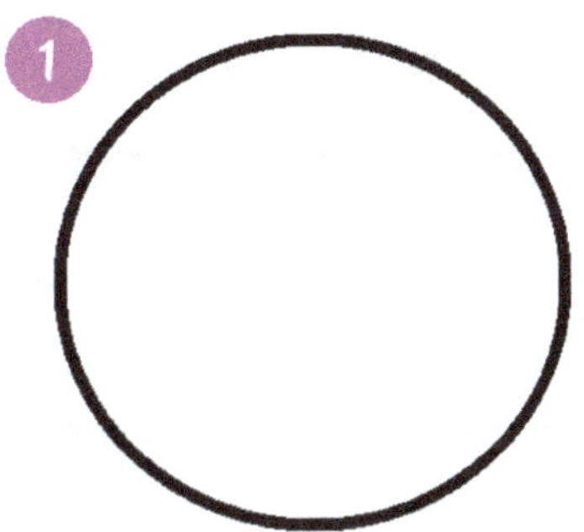

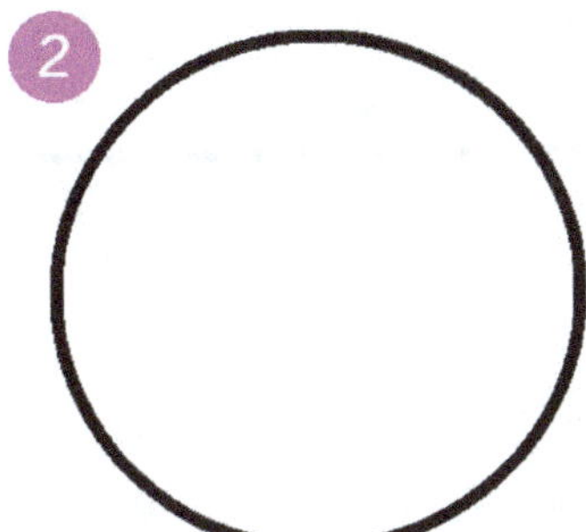

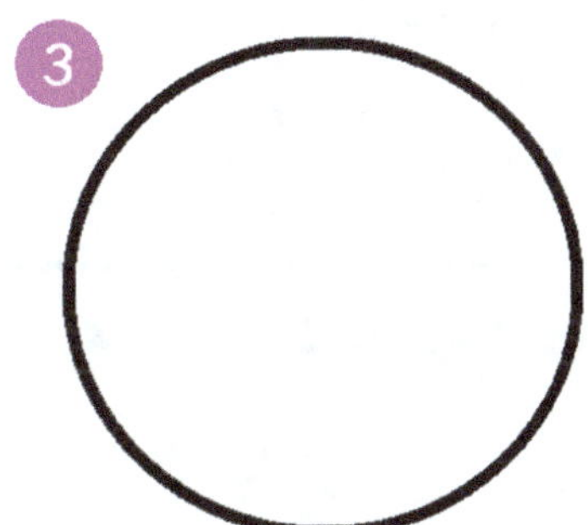

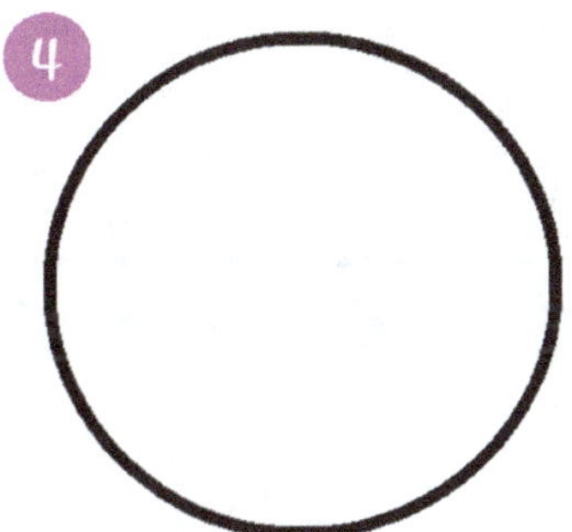

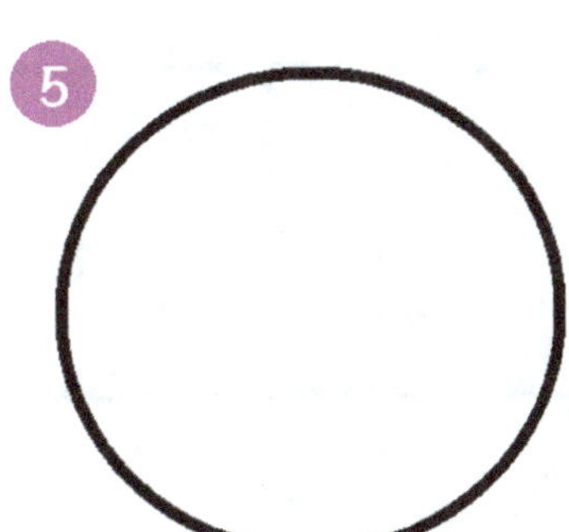

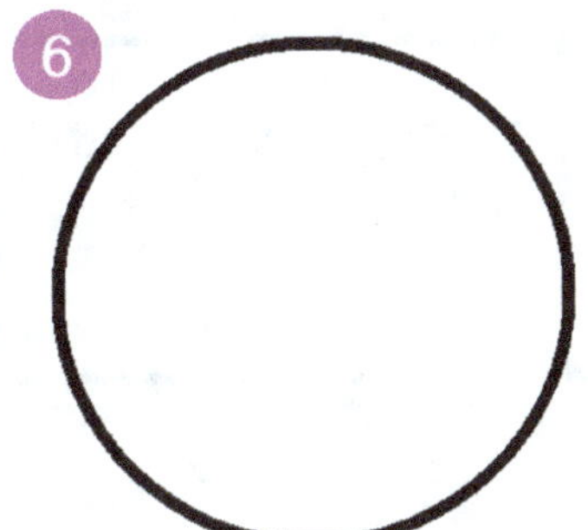 

Write the letter to match the picture

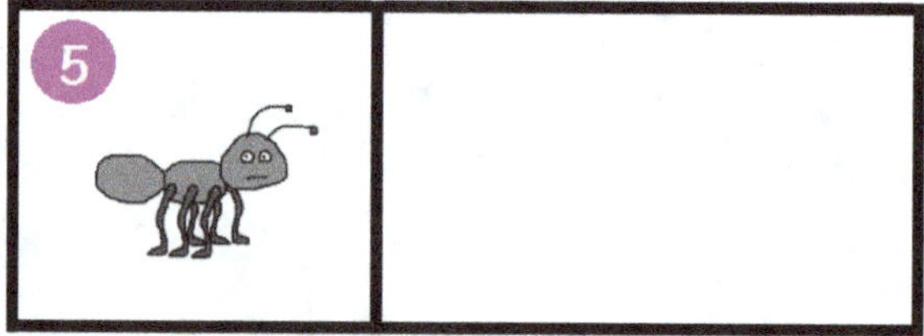

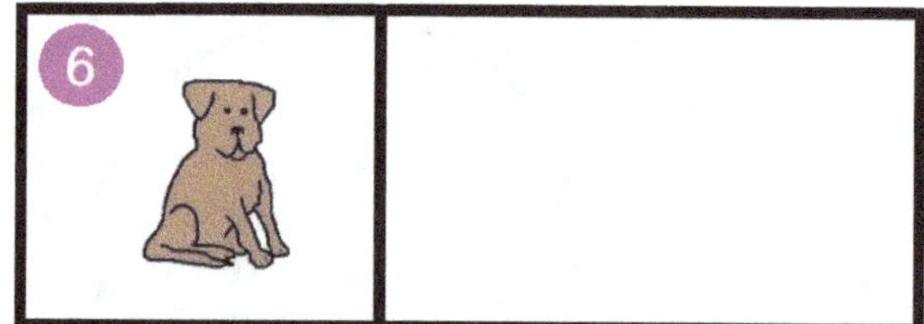

Listen and circle the sound you hear   a Track 84 b Track 85 c Track 86

Tracks 80-87

1 
j c f w y

2 
v g n d i

3 
o h x s t

4 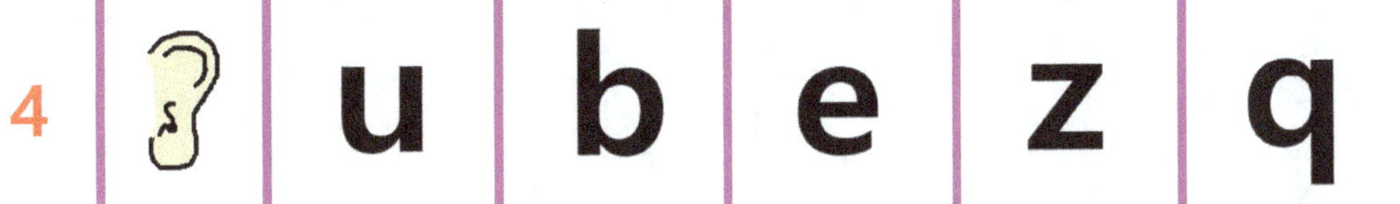
u b e z q

5 
p k m r a

CONGRATULATIONS!

Now you know your alphabet sounds..

You can sing the

Alphabet Sound Song!!

Listen and sing along..if you can!

Tracks 80-87

Track 87

a b c d e f g

h i j k  

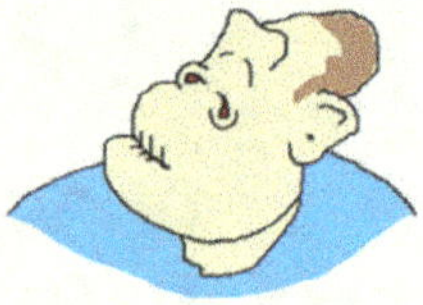

l m n o p

q r s t u v

w x y and z

How did you do?

This is the end of the book!

Word List

Unit 1

alligator   angry   ant   apple

baby   banana   bird   book

candy   car   cat   cup

Unit 2

desk   diamond   dog   door

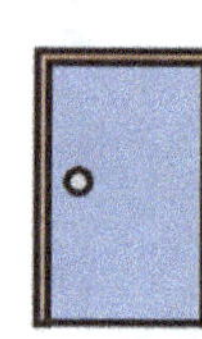

egg   elbow   elephant   elf

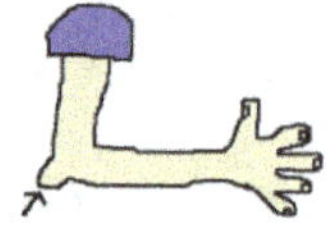

fish   flower   four   frog

Word List

Unit 3

gold

good

gorilla

grass

happy

hat

hill

house

igloo

ill

in

insect

Unit 4

jail

jam

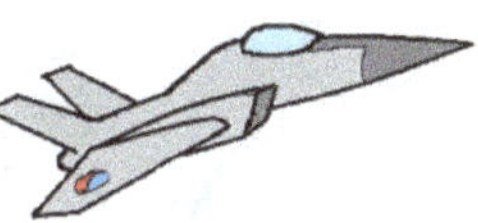
jet

jump

kangaroo

key

kick

kite

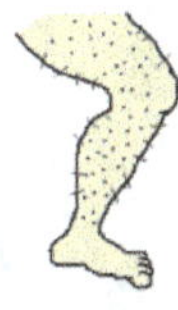
leg

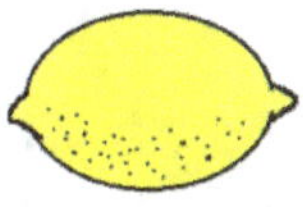
lemon

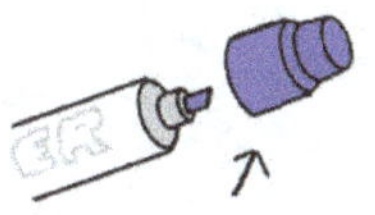
lid

lion

Word List

Unit 5

milk

monkey

moon

mouse

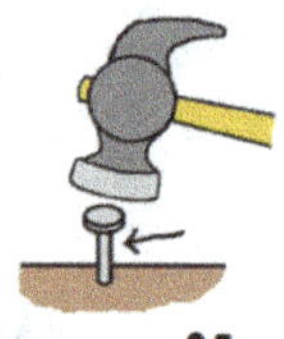
nail

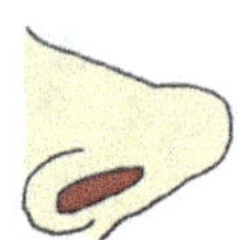
nose

nurse

nut

octopus

old

ox

ostrich

Unit 6

pants

peach

poop

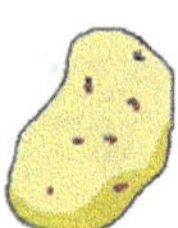
potato

queen

question

quick

quiet

radio

red

robot

run

Word List

Unit 7

sad

sit

smell

sun

tear

ten

tiger

time

umbrella

umpire

under

up

van

vest

violin

vomit

Unit 8

water

wave

window

wish

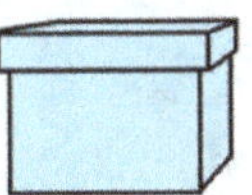
box

fix

fox

six

yawn

yellow

young

yo-yo

zebra

zero

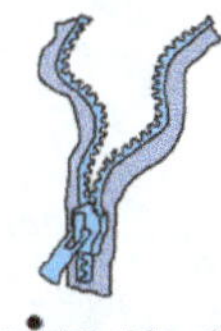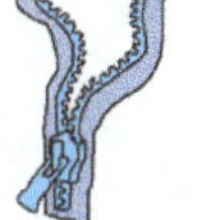
zipper

zoo

What's this page here for?

Well, those flashcards had
to start on a odd page, and
we had no content for this
page.

OUR SIGHT WORD FLASH CARDS!

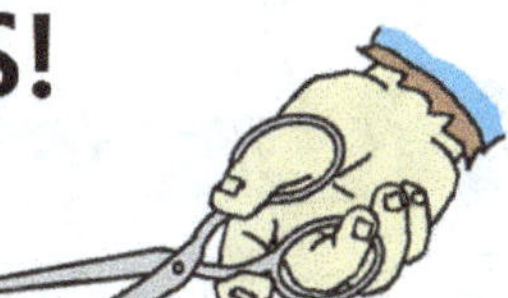

a / an	and
all	on
in	the

OUR SIGHT WORD FLASH CARDS!

no	**lift**
like	**get**
oh	**not**

did

you

your

has

put

one

by	fellow
says	go
to	win

OUR SIGHT WORD FLASH CARDS!

I

had

it

wait

Phonics Series

Preschool:

  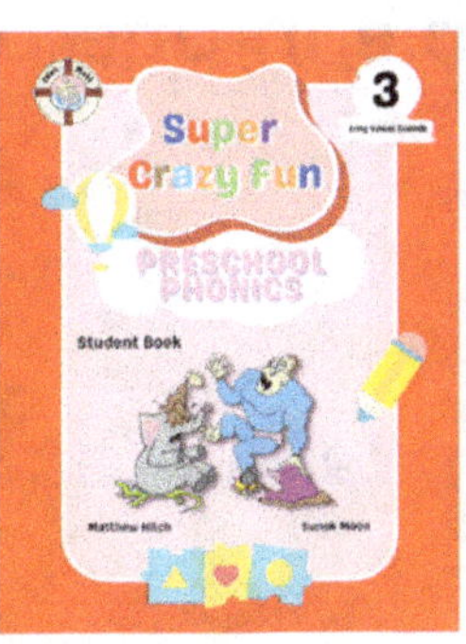  

Kindergarten:

Elementary School Junior:

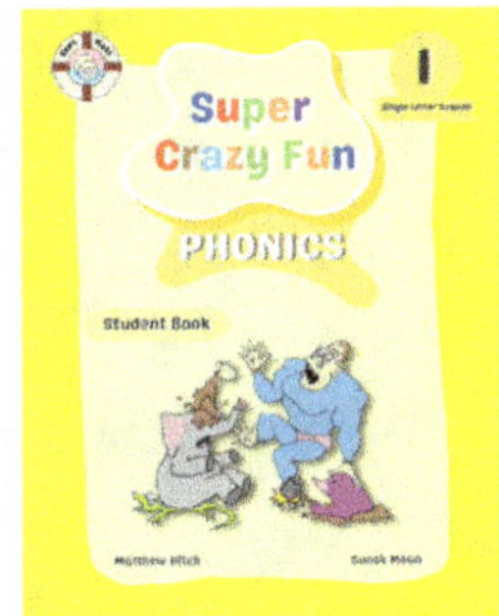  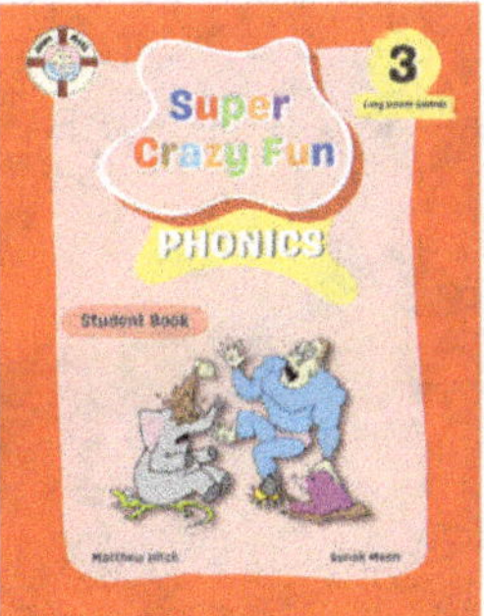 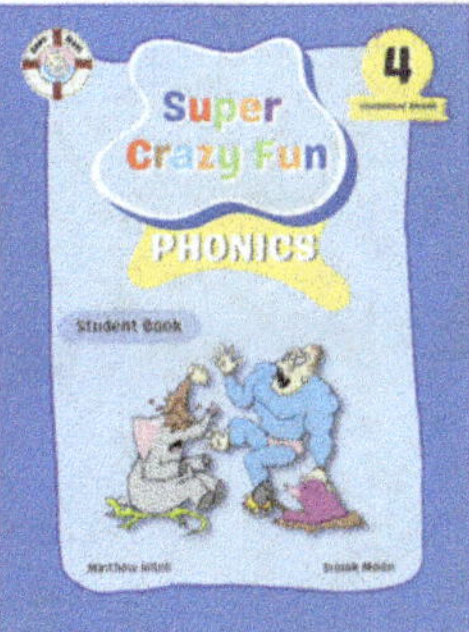 

Elementary School Senior/Remedial:

Incidentally, the contents of all these phonics books are available in one big silly book, too:

Have a look in Amazon or check our website: www.supercrazyfun.net (or just search online in case our publishing options have increased since this was printed.)

There's nothing on this page...